Fishes of the Central United States

Fishes

of the Central United States

JOSEPH R. TOMELLERI & MARK E. EBERLE

ILLUSTRATIONS BY JOSEPH R. TOMELLERI

FOREWORD BY FRANK CROSS

UNIVERSITY PRESS OF KANSAS

© 1990 by the University Press of Kansas
Illustrations © Joseph R. Tomelleri
All rights reserved

Publication made possible in part by grants from the Max McGraw Wildlife Foundation and the Kansas Department of Wildlife and Parks.

Published by the University Press of Kansas (Lawrence, Kansas 66049), which was organized by the Kansas Board of Regents and is operated and funded by Emporia State University, Fort Hays State University, Kansas State University, Pittsburg State University, the University of Kansas, and Wichita State University

Illustration on title page: Brook trout, spawning male

Library of Congress Cataloging-in-Publication Data
Tomelleri, Joseph R.
  Fishes of the central United States / Joseph R. Tomelleri and Mark E. Eberle ; illustrations by Joseph R. Tomelleri ; foreword by Frank Cross.
     p.   cm.
  Includes bibliographical references.
  ISBN 0-7006-0457-X. —ISBN 0-7006-0458-8 (pbk.)
    1. Fishes, Fresh-water—Middle West.   2. Fishes, Fresh-water—Great Plains.   3. Fishing—Middle West.   4. Fishing—Great Plains.
  I. Eberle, Mark E.   II. Title.
QL628.M53T66   1990
597.092'978—dc20   89-38658
                           CIP

Printed in the United States of America

Color plates printed in Hong Kong

10 9 8 7 6 5 4 3

This book is printed on acid-free paper.

To the memory of August A. "Gus" Tomelleri, the "Hudson River piscator," without whose patience, support, and unbridled encouragement this project could not have been completed.

And to the memory of Cyri Marie Eberle, the "lady of the lakes," a Minnesota native whose love of nature and people continues to provide support and inspiration.

Contents

Foreword

FRANK CROSS

The central part of North America is home to the most taxonomically diverse array of freshwater fishes on earth. Other regions, especially in the tropics, have more species, but none has so broad a mix of primitive and derived fishes as the area covered by this book. Joe Tomelleri and Mark Eberle discuss this rich variety through descriptive accounts and illustrations of more than 120 species in 30 families that comprise nearly all the distinctive groups of fish found in the inland waters of the United States. Species likely to be caught by anglers are covered comprehensively; the sunfishes and other game fish are represented abundantly, including several hybrid forms; but such fishes as suckers, sturgeons, minnows, and gars are also well represented.

The accounts of families and species are accurate but not technical, drawn from many sources in the scientific and sportfishing literature and from the authors' own experience. This is an intellectually satisfying lay publication, offering entertainment and enlightenment at a level as appropriate to the coffee table as to the bait shop. Its text is in large degree a framework for Tomelleri's superb illustrations. These are drawings in a classic style that portray anatomical detail faithfully but unobtrusively without sacrificing the essence of the organism as a whole. Tomelleri's work reflects precise observation, disciplined artistic talent, and a fundamental empathy with the subject fishes.

Each kind of fish differs from every other kind in many subtle ways, evident to an ichthyologist but impossible to communicate verbally. Seldom can the whole complement of characters that distinguish a species be captured photographically. Only a drawing can fully reveal the ensemble of features that define a species, but few artists achieve that objective consistently. Tomelleri succeeds in doing so equally well for such varied fishes as trouts, catfishes, sunfishes, pikes, suckers, sticklebacks, silversides, and sculpins. His rapid development as an illustrator is remarkable, as is the way this book has come about.

As students of biology at Fort Hays (Kansas) State University in 1983, Eberle and Tomelleri wondered what kinds of fish might persist in a stream on campus, out of a number of species that were recorded there a century ago. The stream is called Big Creek, a name more appropriate to its 163-mile length than to its dwindling flow, now only a fraction of its former volume. Big Creek exhibited the sort of environmental deterioration that commonly enhances college students' appreciation for aquatic life and calls for investigation—as it did with the authors. After two years' study of Big Creek and its fishes, they published their results, including Tomelleri's first artistic efforts, in 1985. The two then decided to work toward a volume featuring all the large fishes native to Kansas. During the next several months Tomelleri spent one day each week in research collections at the University of Kansas Museum of Natural History, examining photographic slides and specimens of many species. He measured their many dimensions, counted scales, fin rays, and other elements, and sketched them freehand. After completing his drawings, he returned for criticism and correction until morphometric and meristic precision emerged naturally. Ultimately, he concluded that acceptable final illustrations would have to be based on living examples of each kind of fish.

So he and Eberle and associates from their college days became intermittent vagabonds, collecting, sketching, and photographing fishes. Following those travels, Tomelleri spent, on average, about 30 hours completing each of the 163 drawings that appear in this book. The species included were captured from the Montana Rockies to Wisconsin marshes, from Kansas plains to the Missouri Ozarks, and from New Mexico desert streams to East Texas cypress swamps. With the authors' informative narrative these illustrations present a unique, highly attractive survey of the fish fauna of the midcontinental United States.

Preface

There is certainly no shortage of books about fishes. Yet none cover our geographic area specifically, and only a few show any semblance of interest in the little fishes, concentrating instead on the larger, more important economic species. Therefore, we have included both game and nongame fishes in a compendium that strives to be scientifically accurate yet wholly interesting and readable. We present interesting natural histories, historical perspectives, and some of the rich and varied folklores of our fishes.

During the preparation of this work, we decided that if the fishes were to be accurately illustrated in color, they had to be seen in life, "in the field." Therefore, the artist traveled some 16,000 miles to capture fishes in New Mexico, Texas, Arkansas, Montana, Oklahoma, Kansas, Missouri, Iowa, Nebraska, South Dakota, and Wisconsin. Immediately upon collection, the target species were photographed and notes were recorded on life colors. All but the largest fishes were preserved for scale counts, fin ray counts, and measurements to ensure that the drawings would be technically accurate.

The illustrations are intended to show the range of shapes and colors within each species of fish. Whenever Mother Nature, blind luck, and time have permitted, illustrations of both male and female fish have been included, lest the reader grow to believe that sunfishes, darters, and minnows exist only as colorful breeding males. Included in our fish portraits are species that have not previously been illustrated in color and a few fishes that have never been illustrated at all.

The color of a specific fish can vary from day to day, depending on stress, lighting (natural or artificial), water temperature, spawning condition, clarity of the water, and even the viewer's vantage point. Fishes frequently lose their natural colors when placed in an aquarium (sunfishes are the worst offenders). As a result, our illustrations are based upon the appearance of the fishes "in hand," which is how most of us view them. Some of the smaller, nondescript minnows that hold their natural colors for a considerable time were drawn from life whenever time and logistics permitted.

The drawings were executed with Berol Prismacolor and Verithin pencils on six-ply, 100 percent cotton rag museum board. Most of the original drawings approximate life size, although most of the minnows and other small fishes were drawn larger than life to facilitate detailing. Some of the larger fishes, such as the pike and salmons, took about 50 hours of drawing, and the smallest of the minnows took about 12 to 15 hours each to complete.

Our hope is that this volume will stimulate the reader to an appreciation of the incredible diversity and the sometimes brilliant, often subtle beauty of the fishes swimming in our waters.

Joseph R. Tomelleri

Mark E. Eberle

Hays, Kansas
June 1988

Acknowledgments

We are indebted to Frank B. Cross at the University of Kansas for his expertise and encouraging suggestions with all phases of preparation. Dr. Cross reviewed the manuscript, constructively criticized the drawings, helped with identification of many fishes, lent valuable references, and made himself available for many hours of discussion about fishes. Thomas L. Wenke, Fort Hays State University, also offered helpful criticism of drawings, gave much good advice, and put his own knowledge and personal library at our disposal.

We owe a great debt to the photographic skills and many hard hours of fieldwork contributed by Guy W. Ernsting of Natural Science Research Associates and William J. Stark of Oklahoma State University, whose unrestrained enthusiasm helped with the collecting of many of the hard-to-find fishes. Many others also helped to catch fishes, including Bruce Zamrzla and Steve Price of the Kansas Department of Wildlife and Parks; Mike Hatch of the New Mexico Department of Game and Fish; Barney Geyer of Ellis, Kansas; Arthur "Preacher" Ray and his grandson Jason in Zavalla, Texas; David Spiller of Sheboygan, Wisconsin; the Kulpa Fish Company in Two Rivers, Wisconsin; Captain Jon Budge of the *Prompt Delivery*, Port Washington, Wisconsin; Mike Mason of the Iowa Department of Natural Resources; Jim Schroeder of Ainsworth, Nebraska; Dick Ford and his "coldwater fish crew" of the South Dakota Game, Fish, and Parks Department in Rapid City, South Dakota; and James C. Stroh of Hays, Kansas, who also reviewed the manuscript.

The many other individuals who shared their expertise and enabled us to find certain fishes "in the field" include Ken Brunson and Troy Schroeder of the Kansas Department of Wildlife and Parks; Bob Thomas and Larry Hutchinson of the Nebraska Game and Parks Commission; Jim Mayhew of the Iowa Department of Natural Resources; James Fry, William Pflieger, Charles Purkett, and Ron McCullough of the Missouri Department of Conservation; Paul Seidensticker, Dick Luebke, Bob Howells, and George C. Adams of the Texas Department of Wildlife and Parks; Jim McNelly of the Wisconsin Department of Natural Resources; and Gary Marrone, Art Talsma, Robert Hanten, and Larry Firber of the South Dakota Game, Fish, and Parks Department.

Joseph T. Collins and E. O. Wiley at the University of Kansas helped with various aspects of preparation. Eugene D. Fleharty, Robert A. Nicholson, and the Department of Biology at Fort Hays State University helped supply much-needed facilities. Jerry R. Choate of the Museum of the High Plains, Fort Hays State University, assisted with the manuscript and other aspects of publication. The world records were compiled by the National Freshwater Fishing Hall of Fame in Hayward, Wisconsin.

We acknowledge the logistical support provided by Carol M. Dengel, William J. Vogrin, Hugh and Cyri Eberle, and Jay and Lisa Gordon. We are also grateful to Jeanne M. Tomelleri, who assisted in many ways and contributed much time and money, enabling us to complete the project on schedule.

J.R.T.
M.E.E.

External Anatomy of Fishes

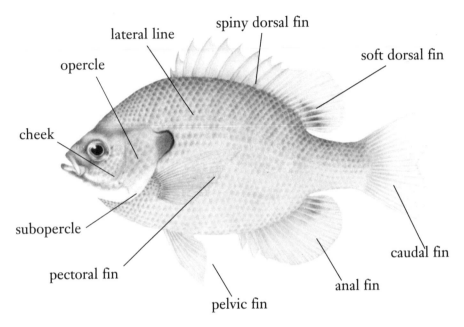

Bluegill, non-breeding male

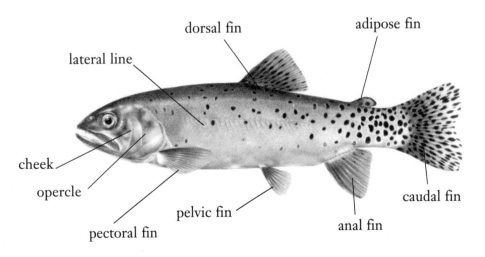

Rio Grande cutthroat

Introduction

This book is an introduction to the freshwater fishes that inhabit the Ozarks and the vast prairie regions between the foothills of the Rocky Mountains and the Mississippi River. This geographic area includes all or part of fifteen states, but most of the fishes presented here have distributions that spread beyond the Great Plains. More than 120 kinds of fishes in thirty families are included. Although the text and its one hundred sixty-five pictures are technically accurate, the book is not intended as an identification manual; our objective in writing it was to entertain and enlighten, whether the reader be a scientist, an angler, or a student of natural history. Therefore the text accompanying the illustrations goes beyond descriptions of identifying characteristics and includes brief accounts of the natural history as well as anecdotes and other notes about each species or group of allied species. Because courtship and spawning habits are so important not only to the fish themselves but also to us as observers, we have described these aspects of the life cycle in a fair amount of detail.

Some of our information is excerpted from the "old masters" of ichthyology, including Constantine Rafinesque, David Starr Jordan, and George Browne Goode, naturalists who discovered the fascinating characteristics–and sometimes indeed created the distinctive personality characterizations–of many American fishes. Readers who seek more detailed accounts of a fish or need help with identification are encouraged to consult the older manuals or one of the state fish books available about the fishes in their area. We have drawn extensively on these publications as well as on our own field experiences in compiling general information about the habits and life histories of our species, and we are greatly indebted to the thousands of researchers who have studied the fishes of North America. These sources are listed in the bibliography, as are many classic references that we have found to be interesting and informative.

Most of our derivations and translations of scientific names were taken from David Starr Jordan and Barton W. Evermann's 1896 monograph, *Fishes of North and Middle America.* The collection of colloquial names is by no means complete; they were selected from scores of books and other publications and from insights provided by the anglers we met in the field. The *Atlas of North American Freshwater Fishes* (Lee et al., 1980) was an invaluable reference in helping to determine the ranges of many species.

The fishes included in our book are not the only species found in the Great Plains, but they provide a reasonably comprehensive portrait of the fish fauna. Over two hundred species of fishes live in the central United States; about fifty of these are shiners (genus *Notropis*) and forty are darters (*Etheostoma* and *Percina*). A few groups of fishes whose ranges include the central United States are not represented in this compilation because they are peripherally distributed or rarely encountered. Among these are the cavefishes (Amblyopsidae), pygmy sunfishes (*Elassoma*), sand darters (*Ammocrypta*), and a half-dozen genera of minnows.

The central United States, as we have defined it, is drained principally by tributaries of the Mississippi River and other

Gulf Coast drainage basins. These include the Missouri, Platte, Kansas, Arkansas, and Red rivers of the Mississippi River system; the Pecos River and Rio Grande of Texas and New Mexico; and the Guadalupe, Colorado, Brazos, and Sabine drainages of Texas and Louisiana. Smaller areas of the central United States are drained by the Great Lakes (the area south and west of Lakes Superior and Michigan) and Hudson Bay, which includes the Red River of the North.

Within these drainages are some distinct physiographic provinces that harbor different assemblages of fishes. Our native trout waters are the cold, clear brooks and rivers of northeast Iowa and southeastern Minnesota, but cutthroat trout are native just to the west of the High Plains in the mountain headwaters of the Missouri drainage in Wyoming and Montana and in the South Platte system of northeast Colorado and southeast Wyoming. Although the frigid waters of the Black Hills in South Dakota have few native fishes, the streams are ideally suited to several species of introduced trouts, including the brown, brook, and rainbow trouts. The pristine streams of the Missouri and Arkansas Ozarks are astoundingly clear (one can see 15 feet deep on a good day) and support our most diverse fish faunas, including several species of darters that are found nowhere else in the world. The Edwards Plateau of south-central Texas is also largely unspoiled; it has a peculiar assemblage of fishes among its subtropical array of sparkling rivers and creeks.

These unique waters and their faunas, as well as the other aquatic communities

throughout the Great Plains, pose some interesting and difficult problems with respect to conservation and proper management of both the fishes and their habitats. Modifications of the environment in the central United States have had both negative and positive impacts on the aquatic resource.

Various perturbations now threaten all or part of the ranges of several species of fishes on the Great Plains. For instance, the quality and quantity of water in our lakes and streams have deteriorated in many parts of the Great Plains. This is principally a result of groundwater depletion and conservation practices that have reduced runoff and streamflows and of agricultural practices that have resulted in silty streambeds and turbid water. Our waters have also been exposed to hazardous levels of chemicals from various sources. Additionally, the construction of dams has blocked the migration of some fishes and inundated the spawning or feeding habitats of others. Introductions of fishes, such as the common carp and the mosquitofish, also have adversely affected populations of native fishes through habitat alteration and competition. Even introduced populations of the popular smallmouth bass have threatened the existence of the guadalupe bass through hybridization.

Yet the outlook for other fishes in the central United States is positive. Despite much negative impact on native fishes from dam construction, some species have benefited from impoundments. For instance, below dams the level of turbidity of rivers is reduced because the silt settles out in the slack waters of the reservoir. As a result, some species with low tolerances of turbidity, such as the skipjack herring, have expanded their ranges into these stream reaches. Also, some species native to stream pools have increased in abundance in these large artificial "pools." Dams can also help maintain minimum desirable stream flows during periods of drought.

The most important change affecting fishes and their habitats, however, is probably economic, not environmental. The multibillion dollar sportfishing industry generates fees and taxes that are used to enhance fishing opportunities. In many instances these monies have sponsored comprehensive management programs that benefit nongame animals as well as game fishes and their habitats. The public's growing concern for the conservation of the entire system of natural resources means that several state conservation agencies have now supplemented their treasuries with money from tax check-off donations. Missouri has even devoted a small portion of the state sales tax to conservation.

What all of these changes boil down to is an understanding that although some alterations of the aquatic resource are inevitable, the integrity of the natural environment must be considered paramount. Within the central United States, all of the states except Louisiana have compiled a list of fish species that are protected or of special concern. Species are added to these lists from time to time, but they are also taken off as their populations become stable, either by chance or by design. Not all species will be so fortunate, but it is not unreasonable to expect that a place can be found in nature for the vast majority. There is an amazing amount of diversity among the fishes of the central United States, and those who take the time to observe them can learn much of practical and intrinsic value. We have derived a great many hours of pleasure from the pursuit of such knowledge, and we hope that this book will help you to do the same.

Lampreys

Family PETROMYZONTIDAE

When you were a tadpole and I was a fish,
In the Paleozoic time.
—Langdon Smith
  Evolution

Chestnut Lamprey

Ichthyomyzon castaneus

Plates 1–2

Colloquial names: hitchhiker, lamprey eel, brown lamprey, bloodsucker, seven-eyed cat, western lamprey, lamper

Scientific name:
Ichthyomyzon, Greek for "fish sucker"
castaneus, Greek for "chestnut color"

Distribution: Occurring in much of central North America, principally in the lower Mississippi River and its tributaries. Absent from the High Plains.

Size: Commonly 6–8 inches, to a maximum of 12 inches.

Status: Several species of parasitic and nonparasitic (brook) lampreys are of special concern in some parts of the central United States.

The lampreys are relics of an ancient group of fishes that lived some 350 million years ago. Taxonomically speaking, lampreys have been on a "slow boat to China" for millions of years and consequently have no relatives among any of our freshwater fishes. A lamprey superficially resembles an eel but is unique for its circular, sucking mouth, lack of pectoral fins, and the seven gill "pores" along each side of its head. Lampreys are cartilaginous, slender, and slippery and upon their capture will wriggle incessantly, being virtually impossible to hold in the hand unless the captor can coax them to suck tightly (albeit temporarily) onto a finger or palm.

The life cycle of the lamprey comprises distinct immature and adult stages. Larval lampreys, called ammocoetes, were once mistakenly classified as adult lampreys in their own genus of the same name. The larvae are nonparasitic, have a horseshoe-shaped mouth, and have no functional eyes. The ammocoetes burrow into silt or muddy stream bottoms where they strain organic material from the water. The chestnut lamprey requires two or three years to complete its larval development, at which time it ceases to feed and transforms into an adult. The adult lamprey feeds by "sucking" onto a catfish, carp, or other large host fish. Using its hard, toothed "tongue," the lamprey rasps away scales and skin on the side of the fish and feeds on blood and body fluids for several days before detaching. This feeding cycle continues for about six months in the chestnut lamprey. Host fishes are usually not killed by the lamprey, but infections often develop as a result of the wound.

Lampreys spawn in gravel "pits" in shallow, clean riffles of small streams. Most lampreys have decreased in abundance over the last forty years because of siltation and dewatering of many of their former spawning sites.

Our lampreys include several parasitic species and four species of nonparasitic brook lampreys. The chestnut lamprey is the most commonly encountered species in our region. The parasitic sea lamprey, which entered the Great Lakes via the Welland Ship Canal (partially by "hitchhiking" on ship's hulls), devastated lake trout populations in the 1940s and 1950s before being brought under control with chemicals and electrical weirs.

Sturgeons

Family ACIPENSERIDAE

Differs from the Sturgeon, by having two dorsal and no abdominal fins. First dorsal anterior, the second opposed to the anal. This genus rests altogether upon the authority of Mr. Audubon, who has presented me a drawing of the only species belonging to it. It appears very distinct if his drawing be correct; but it requires to be examined again. Is it only a Sturgeon incorrectly drawn?
—Constantine Rafinesque, 1820
    Ichthyologia Ohiensis
    describing the Flatnose Doublefin, a
    "species" contrived by John James Audubon

The sturgeons are an ancient group of fishes consisting of about 25 species worldwide. Sturgeons have a primitive but flexible cartilaginous skeleton, and their sides are protected by rows of sharp, bony plates (called scutes) rather than the typical scales. Their spindle-shaped, streamlined bodies and small eyes are well adapted to life in the turbid mainstreams of our major rivers. Sturgeons spend much of their time gliding over the bottoms of rivers and lakes in search of aquatic insects, crayfish, mussels, or fish. Their odd tubular and protrusile mouths are used like a vacuum cleaner to inhale their prey. Some species of sturgeons are harvested for their highly prized flesh and for their eggs, which are the principle source of caviar. In Russia, the sturgeons are the most valuable of all market fishes and are used for cured filet (*balyk*), "Russian" caviar, and *vyaziga*, a derivative of the cartilaginous axial skeleton.

Sturgeons are slow to grow and mature, but they are relatively long lived, which enables them to be among the largest freshwater fishes. Both the white sturgeon of our Pacific Coast and the Beluga of Russia approached lengths of 20 feet and weights of 2000 pounds in the nineteenth century. The slow growth rate of sturgeons and the length of time required for them to reach sexual maturity (perhaps 20 years for lake sturgeons) make them sensitive to overharvesting. Their future in the central United States and elsewhere has dimmed somewhat in the last century, in part a result of overfishing and pollution. Developments along our major waterways, including dams and channelization, also have interfered with the success of our sturgeons, and two of the three species found in the central United States are now protected by many states.

Lake Sturgeon

Acipenser fulvescens

Plate 3

Colloquial names: dogface sturgeon, rock sturgeon, rubbernose sturgeon, red sturgeon, black sturgeon, shellback sturgeon, ruddy sturgeon

Scientific name:
Acipenser, Latin for "sturgeon"
fulvescens, Latin for "reddish-yellow"

Distribution: Native to the Great Lakes, Mississippi River, and Hudson Bay drainages. Rare throughout the Mississippi drainage; still common in portions of Wisconsin and Canada.

Size: The largest of our sturgeons, reaching 5 feet in length and a weight of 80 pounds. Formerly, the species grew to 200–300 pounds. The world record for hook-and-line weighed 92 lbs. 4 oz. and was caught in the Kettle River of Minnesota in 1986.

Status: Protected or of special concern in most of its range in the Mississippi Valley. Currently being reintroduced into Missouri.

Lake sturgeons, among the largest fishes in the central United States, are typically found in water 15–30 feet deep over the muddy-bottomed shoals of lakes and large rivers. Lake sturgeons feed on the bottom with the aid of their sensory barbels, "sucking up" any edibles with their protrusile mouths. Because of their feeding habits, lake sturgeons are sometimes blamed for consuming the eggs of sport fishes, a largely unfounded assertion since the muddy feeding areas are not good spawning sites for most sport fishes.

Lake sturgeons are slow to mature and typically will not reproduce until after their twelfth year of life. They migrate upstream into small, swiftly flowing rivers to spawn and will also breed over the rocky, wave-swept shallows of lakes, often with their snouts, backs, or tails protruding from the water. Spawning intervals vary; mature males might breed every second or third year, but females reproduce only once every four to six years. Because of their sporadic spawning and long drawn-out "adolescence," lake sturgeons are particularly vulnerable to overharvesting. Females grow more slowly but live longer than males; consequently the majority of individuals over 50 years of age are females. Lake sturgeons are known to reach 150 years of age.

Although prior to 1860 North American fishermen considered the lake sturgeon to be useful only as pig fodder or fertilizer, Scott and Crossman, in their *Freshwater Fishes of Canada,* reported a more enterprising utility of the lake sturgeon—the species was once dried and stacked on docks for use as fuel in steamships that sailed the Detroit River! Eventually, the commercial value of the fish's meat and eggs (used for caviar) led to overharvesting of the lake sturgeon in the early 1900s. Commercial and sport harvest of this species are now strictly regulated in some states.

Shovelnose Sturgeon

Scaphirhynchus platorynchus

Plate 4

Colloquial names: hackleback, switchtail, sand sturgeon, duck-billed cat, flathead sturgeon

Scientific name:
Scaphirhynchus, Greek for "spade snout"
platorynchus, Greek for "broad snout"

Distribution: Mississippi and Missouri rivers and larger tributaries, occurring as far west as Montana and Wyoming via the Missouri and Platte rivers. A disjunct population once occurred in the Rio Grande of northern New Mexico.

Size: Averaging about 20 inches and 1.5 pounds, to a maximum of about 5 pounds. A 13 lb. 11 oz. specimen was caught in Montana in 1986.

Status: Taken by commercial fishermen and anglers in some areas. Within the central United States, it is protected or of special concern in Minnesota, North Dakota, Texas, and Wyoming.

The most common sturgeon in the rivers of the central United States, shovelnose sturgeons usually are found over sandy river bottoms in strong current. Except for the pallid sturgeon, the only other "shovelnosed" sturgeons live in rivers that empty into the Aral Sea of the southern Soviet Union.

Relatively little is known about the spawning habits of the shovelnose sturgeon. Reaching maturity at five to seven years of age, it apparently spawns in the river channel over a rocky substrate. The food of shovelnose sturgeons is similar to that of the other freshwater sturgeons, consisting principally of aquatic invertebrates that it sucks from the stream bottom. The species is occasionally caught by fishermen who bottom-fish worms for catfish.

Like other sturgeons, the young shovelnose has a long, threadlike extension of cartilaginous backbone that trails from the upper lobe of the caudal fin. This "whiptail" is prone to breakage and is usually much reduced or absent in adult sturgeons.

Pallid Sturgeon

Scaphirhynchus albus

Plate 5

Colloquial names: white hackleback, white sturgeon, white shovelnose

Scientific name:
Scaphirhynchus, Greek for "spade snout" *albus*, Latin for "white"

Distribution: Missouri River and the Mississippi River below St. Louis.

Size: Growing to about 40 pounds. The world record weighed 49 lbs. 8 oz. and was caught in the Missouri River in North Dakota in 1984.

Status: Threatened throughout much of its range, it is protected or of special concern in Iowa, Kansas, Missouri, Montana, Nebraska, North Dakota, and South Dakota within the central United States. Most common in our range in Montana and the Dakotas. A candidate for federal listing as an endangered species.

Little is known about the pallid sturgeon, for the species is only rarely observed and is infrequently taken on hook-and-line. Even the historical records of the species are obscure because it was not formally distinguished from the shovelnose sturgeon until 1905. The pallid sturgeon shares with its look-alike cousin a preference for the strong currents of sandy-bottomed rivers. The pallid sturgeon is much less common than the shovelnose, but interestingly, seems to be more tolerant of turbidity. Like other sturgeons, the pallid sturgeon feeds on bottom-dwelling organisms, but some researchers suggest that the pallid sturgeon consumes a greater percentage of fish than its shovelnosed congener.

Both the pallid and shovelnose sturgeons occur together throughout much of the Missouri River. Both species are taken by anglers, but the shovelnose is by far the more frequently caught. The two species are similar in appearance, but the belly of the pallid sturgeon is smooth, whereas that of the adult shovelnose is covered with bony plates (scutes). Also, the four barbels ("whiskers") of the pallid sturgeon are staggered, with the two relatively short center barbels originating slightly closer to the front of the snout than those of the shovelnose sturgeon, whose barbels are about equal in length and are set in a straight line.

Paddlefishes

Family POLYODONTIDAE

I want you gentlemen on the other side of the
House to "fish or cut bait!"
—Joseph G. Cannon
U.S. House of Representatives, 1876

Paddlefish

Polyodon spathula
Plate 6

Colloquial names: duckbilled cat, shovel-billed cat, spoonbilled cat, oarfish, spade-fish, spatula fish

Scientific name:
Polyodon, Greek for "many tooth" (probably in reference to the many gill rakers, for the paddlefish is actually toothless)
spathula, Latin for "spatula" or "blade"

Distribution: Occurring in most larger rivers in the Mississippi River drainage, to western Montana in the Missouri River.

Size: Commonly reaching 30 pounds in weight. The world record paddlefish weighed 142 lbs. 8 oz. and was snagged in the Missouri River of Montana in 1973.

Status: Sport fish. Reduced over much of its range because of dams and the subsequent inundation of many spawning grounds. Protected or of special concern in about a dozen states. In the central United States these include Minnesota, Montana, North Dakota, South Dakota, and Texas.

Despite the large size, gaping mouth, and strange, unmistakable appearance of the prehistoric paddlefish, it is no "monster." In fact, this gentle giant feeds only on tiny plankton that it collects with its large, toothless mouth. Although the utility of its long, flat snout is largely unknown, some scientists have suggested the so-called paddle is used to stir up small organisms in bottom sediments. Taste buds on the paddlefish's snout and head also help it to locate concentrations of its microscopic food.

The paddlefish inhabits larger rivers in the Mississippi Basin and a few other Gulf Coast drainages. In some areas, the paddlefish's annual spring spawning migration is blocked by dams, and the fish consequently become concentrated. Normally, these are the only times and places where paddlefish can be caught as sport. Because paddlefish feed only on microscopic animals (which are rather difficult to thread on a hook), the usual way to catch paddlefish is by "blind snagging," a sport that utilizes a heavy weight and a large treble hook that are continually jerked through the water in hopes of hooking a fish. The paddlefish is easily chopped into steaks, because the species has "no bones about it." The eggs are sometimes used for caviar, although most marketed caviar comes from sturgeon eggs.

Mr. Allis of the Allis-Chalmers Corporation once offered a reward of $1,000 for the discovery of a paddlefish less than 2 inches long, but the reward was never claimed. The young remained virtually unknown prior to 1932, and the spawning ritual of the paddlefish remained a mystery until 1960, when Charles Purkett of the Missouri Department of Conservation discovered the species breeding along shoals of the Osage River in central Missouri.

Gars

Family LEPISOSTEIDAE

In October when the water starts to cool down,
they school up and break the surface of the
water like a porpoise. I've seen schools of 'gator
gar maybe one-half mile wide and a mile long.
There ain't quite so many now since we thinned
'em. Just ain't natural to have that many
alligator gar in a lake. Found a seven pound
bass in a 'gator gar once."
—*Arthur "Preacher" Ray*
 Zavalla, Texas, 1987

The gars are a primitive group of fishes that are endemic to the fresh and brackish waters of Central and North America. They are outcasts among fishes, having no relatives among any of our species excepting the bowfin, which may be thought of as a distant second cousin. The family has a poor reputation among anglers, who believe gars would have been better suited as land dwellers had they been able to stand their own reflections in the water.

The gars are virtually unchanged from millions of years ago, and their survival from prehistoric times is testament to their novel design. A gar's body is sheathed with an array of enamel-hard, diamond-shaped plates called ganoid scales, a combination proving so impregnable that Caribbeans once used the dried hides for breastplates and the scales as arrowheads.

Especially designed for backwaters, oxbows, and bayous, a gar can breathe both with its gills and with its special lunglike air bladder. The highly vascularized air bladder is connected to its throat, allowing the gar to breathe oxygen much like a mammal does. Thus, gars are equipped to survive in hot, rank, stagnant waters that might not have sufficient oxygen for most other species of fish.

Gars spawn in March and April in the southern states and as late as June in the northern latitudes. No nests are built; instead the female, which is usually much larger than the male, spawns by broadcasting her adhesive eggs in shallow pools, weedy backwaters, or shallow riffles. The greenish-colored eggs (widely held to be poisonous to warm-blooded animals) are fertilized as they are released, usually by two or more attending males. The newly hatched larva has a peculiar adhesive disc on the front of its blunt snout, which it uses to attach itself to gravel or other submerged objects. Young gars have a peculiar, fragile fin that extends along the upper edge of the tail and vibrates constantly. It is lost during the first year of life.

Patience is a virtue for hungry gars. Sometimes a gar will float stealthily along the surface of the water, disguised from all the world as a stick or log. Coming upon a wounded or unwary fish, the gar will propel itself slowly forward with a furtive flick of its fins. Once into position, the gar convulsively snaps its head sideways and secures the prey with its sharp teeth. The gar will then slowly reposition the fish and swallow it head first. Gars commonly take a short swim or "victory lap" after making a catch, as if suspicious of some neighbor's less than honorable intentions.

Gars are among our most misunderstood fishes and because of their voracious feeding habits are sometimes blamed for poor fishing. Actually, gars feed upon gizzard

19

shad to a large extent and benefit sport fish populations by eating mostly sick or weak individuals.

A few anglers enjoy the gars as sport and have developed clever techniques of catching them. Because of the gar's sharp teeth and bony jaws, anglers often opt for a wire leader using shredded nylon floss to entangle the gar's teeth. Another method employs a baited wire noose that is pulled tight over the jaws once the gar has nosed its way into the bait.

Alligator Gar

Lepisosteus spatula

Plate 7

Colloquial names: gator gar, Mississippi alligator gar, great gar, marjuari

Scientific name:
Lepisosteus, Greek for "scale of bone"
spatula, Latin for "spoon," a reference to the broad alligatorlike snout

Distribution: Most abundant in large rivers along the Gulf Coast. A few taken as far north in the Mississippi River as St. Louis, and old records exist from the Illinois and upper Ohio rivers. Young have been found in Lake Texoma in southern Oklahoma.

Size: The largest fish in the central United States, commonly exceeding a length of 7 feet and a weight of 150 pounds, to a documented size of 9 feet 8.5 inches and 302 pounds. The hook-and-line record is 279 pounds, caught from the Rio Grande of Texas in 1951.

Status: Protected or of special concern along the northern limits of its range in Missouri, Illinois, Kentucky, and Tennessee.

The voracious appetite and portentous size of the alligator gar have inspired a fabled collection of anecdotes, folklore, half-truths, and plain facts. Lengths of 15 to 20 feet are attributed to it in undocumented and undoubtedly exaggerated yarns that are still spun in the Texas and Louisiana bayous. But credence cannot be given to these claims even though the well-respected J. R. Norman, in *A History of Fishes,* stated that

> The alligator gar-pike, abundant in the rivers around the Gulf of Mexico, and at-

taining a length of twenty feet or more is very destructive to food fishes, and causes a great deal of damage to the nets of fishermen, who kill it without mercy. It is not even good eating itself, the flesh being rank and tough, and unfit even for dogs.

The alligator gar inhabits estuaries, bayous, and overflow pools along major rivers and eats mostly fishes, but ducks, snakes, muskrats, and any other floating animal might be consumed.

Young alligator gars are occasionally confused with shortnose and spotted gars. The alligator gar can be recognized by its broader head and toothy "crocodile" smile, which is accentuated by the two rows of large teeth in its upper jaws (other gars have two rows only as immatures).

Because of its enormous size, commercial fishermen have adapted the special technique of jugging to the alligator gar. A 2-liter plastic jug is used as a float, and a heavy braided line with a two-pronged hook is tied securely to the jug. A stout 6-foot pole is attached along the length of the line at the jug, to prevent a hooked gar from eating jug and fisherman! A 2-or 3-pound carp or gaspergou (freshwater drum) is used for bait. The set is then tossed into an advantageous area of the reservoir and is allowed to float freely overnight.

The next morning the fisherman goes "spotting" for his jugs, which sometimes have been carried for several miles. Hooked gars will thrash, belch, and jump spectacularly when disturbed, pull the jug deep underwater, and resurface at a considerable distance from the boat. The fisherman will sometimes lasso the jug and add several more floats to the set, making the successive soundings by the gar shorter and more tiring. The exhausted gar is finally pulled cautiously toward the boat and effectively subdued before being boated. Gator gars are skinned using a hatchet, and about one-half the weight will dress out as marketable flesh. Most of the large gars (over 150 pounds) are females, and folklore says that large males are rarely caught because they change their sex once they reach 80 or 90 pounds. As is the case with other gars, the females are probably just longer lived and thus considerably larger than the males. A substantial rod and reel fishery also exists in some of the larger southern rivers, the White River of Arkansas being the most famous.

Dr. Ed Wiley of the University of Kansas is in the process of describing a heretofore unknown species of gar from the Gulf of Mexico coastal plain. The fish is similar in size and appearance to the alligator gar, but its snout is longer and not as broad as the gator gar's. Known from only 10 specimens, the species has in the past been considered a hybrid between the longnose and alligator gars. Because of its preference for coastal waters, Dr. Wiley has christened the species "sea gar," not to be confused with Cuba's cigars.

Longnose Gar

Lepisosteus osseus

Plate 8

Colloquial names: needlenose gar, fish gar, gar-pike, billfish, billy gar, pin-nose gar, bonypike, common gar-pike, scissorbill

Scientific name:
Lepisosteus, Greek for "scale of bone"
osseus, Latin for "of bone"

Distribution: Found throughout the eastern half of the United States along major riverways; absent from the extreme northeast. Into the Great Plains along the Missouri, Arkansas, and Red rivers and into southeast New Mexico via the Rio Grande and the Pecos River.

Size: Frequently attaining a weight of 10 to 15 pounds and a length of 40 inches. The world record longnose, caught in the Trinity River of Texas in 1954, weighed 50 lbs. 5 oz. Experts view the record with circumspection, insisting the fish was actually Dr. Ed Wiley's undescribed "sea gar" (see account of alligator gar).

Status: Not threatened in any state.

The long and slender "needlenose" of the longnose gar is virtually unmistakable, being 15 to 20 times longer than its least width. The longnose gar is our most common and widely distributed gar and is abundant in many of our large reservoirs.

The needle-sharp teeth and incessant smirk of the longnose gar have long been a scourge to anglers. Capture a longnose, and it matter-of-factly smiles upon your misfortune. Toss it upon the bank, and it rewards you with a toothy eye-to-eye grin. For all its durability, this gar seems as much at home on the floor of a flat-bottomed johnboat as in the bayou.

In its exceptional tenacity for life, the gar is a valiant fighter. Once, having captured a longnose, we promptly preserved the fish in an airtight 5-gallon bucket that was half-filled with the usual solution. Upon our arrival home some 90 minutes later, we found the fish still making every effort to escape, having survived the journey and the preservative on the 2.5 gallons of "atmosphere" in the bucket.

The longnose gar is abundant in streams but is more inclined toward sluggish waters than its close relative the shortnose gar. Although occasionally found in swift riffles, the longnose gar is more apt to frequent large, deep pools and the margins of eddies, patiently relying on the current to deliver its food.

We have heard reference in east Texas to a mysterious "blue gar," a fish supposedly indistinguishable from the longnose gar on the basis of external characteristics. Blue gars are supposedly identifiable by the blue tint of their flesh, which is not saleable in commercial markets.

Shortnose Gar

Lepisosteus platostomus

Plate 9

Colloquial names: billy gar, shortbill gar, stubnose gar, duckbilled gar

Scientific name:
Lepisosteus, Greek for "scale of bone"
platostomus, Greek for "broad mouth"

Distribution: Throughout most of the Missouri, Mississippi, and Ohio rivers and their larger tributaries. Abundant in Louisiana and east Texas.

Size: Generally less than 2 feet in length: the smallest of our gar species. The official world record is 3 lbs. 5 oz., but much larger fish have been caught; the Nebraska record is 19 pounds.

Status: Protected or of special concern in Montana, North Dakota, and Ohio.

The shortnose gar is more tolerant of muddy, turbid waters than most other gars and as a result is common in our larger rivers. The shortnose also inhabits oxbows, reservoirs, or other quiet waters where it is sometimes the most abundant species of gar. The shortnose lives principally on a diet of fish but is somewhat more catholic in its tastes than the spotted or longnose gars, frequently feeding upon crayfish and insects.

The broad and stubby snout of the shortnose distinguishes it from the longnose gar. In clear water, however, the shortnose gar sometimes develops poorly defined spots on the top of his head, which might cause it to be confused with the spotted gar. For absolute identification, count the lateral line scales—60 or more in the shortnose and usually 58 or less in the spotted gar.

As in all of our species of gars, the young shortnose carries a black stripe along its midside. Young gars are fast growers and might reach a foot or more in length within their first year of life.

We have taken shortnose gars on occasion in small streams some distance from major rivers. When in clear water, the species has proved to be difficult to catch with any but the largest of seines, oftentimes darting around the net with short explosive thrusts of its hindward fins. In turbid water, the task of capture is easier, and gars are netted with much less effort.

Spotted Gar

Lepisosteus oculatus

Plate 10

Colloquial names: billfish, shortnose gar

Scientific name:
Lepisosteus, Greek for "scale of bone"
oculatus, Latin for "provided with eyes," a
reference to the profusely spotted head and
body

Distribution: Most abundant along the
coastal plains of Texas and Louisiana and
common in the swampy lowlands of Oklahoma, Missouri, and Arkansas. Occurring
sporadically as far north as Lake Erie but
absent from most of Kansas, Missouri, and
the northern Great Plains.

Size: Frequently attaining a length of 3 feet
in the southern states. Generally larger and
more robust than the shortnose gar but
shorter than the longnose gar. The world
record weighed 28 lbs. 8 oz. and was caught
in Lake Seminole, Florida, in 1987.

Status: Threatened or of special concern
in Kansas, Kentucky, and Ohio.

The spotted gar is the only gar in the central United States that consistently sees
"spots before its eyes." Although other gars
are variably spotted on the fins and body,
the spotted gar is the only adult gar with
distinct black blotches on both the snout
and head.

The shortnose and spotted gars are
sometimes difficult to tell apart, especially
immature specimens, and the species were
formerly considered to be conspecific. A
good, though not always reliable characteristic, is the general disposition of their body
shapes. Whereas the cylindrical body of the
shortnose is of a uniform thickness, the
profile of the spotted gar tends to be thick-
est (almost "pot bellied") at its pelvic fins.

As with other family members, the young
of the spotted gar are brightly colored.
Specimens less than 4 inches long are
handsomely groomed with a dark brown
dorsal stripe, a black lateral band with a
narrow reddish stripe above, and a
chocolate-colored belly.

The spotted gar's affinity is for the quiet,
clear, weedy waters of oxbows and lowland
lakes. Go angling in a cypress swamp and
know that this species will not be far behind. Fish the same with minnows or cut
bait and the spotted gars might congregate,
consistently fouling your lines and stealing
your bait, for all the world like uninvited
guests with a penchant for rudeness. Once
we continually caught spotted gars but a
dozen feet from shore by casting minnows
and allowing the gars to swim with the bait,
stop, and swallow before we set the hook.
The species did not seem to be particularly
wary, and we might have captured them all
day long had we not other species to procure.

Bowfins

Family AMIIDAE

The young, when about six inches long, make a famous bait for pickerel and pike. To use it, run the hook into the mouth right up through the center of the head, through the brains, cast a hundred times, catch several fish, and at the end of three to six hours he will kick like a mule.

Put a hundred in a rain-barrel and you can keep them all summer without a change of water.
—Charles Hallock
 Nineteenth-century naturalist

Bowfin

Amia calva

Plates 11–12

Colloquial names: dogfish, grinnel, John A. Grindle, cottonfish, cypress trout, mudfish, blackfish, choupique (in Louisiana, derived from the Choctaw name for bowfin, *shupik*, meaning "mudfish"), lawyer, poisson de marais ("fish of the swamp"), speckled cat, scaled ling

Scientific name:
Amia, the name of a fish in ancient Greece
calva, Latin for "smooth"

Distribution: Ranging over much of the lowlands of the eastern United States. Most common in our range in the sloughs and backwaters of the Mississippi River Valley, from Minnesota to the Gulf of Mexico. Mostly absent from the Great Plains, except as strays in larger rivers.

Size: Commonly 2 to 3 feet in length and 5 to 9 lbs in weight. The world record for hook-and-line weighed 21 lbs. 8 oz. and was caught in Forest Lake, South Carolina, in January 1980.

Status: Sport fish; not protected in any state.

The bowfin is the sole survivor of a prehistoric family of fishes of which fossil remains have been discovered in both Europe and North America. This relict is now found only in lowland waters of the eastern United States and in the Great Lakes region of Canada, where it is uniquely adapted for life in warm, stagnant waters.

Bowfins typically inhabit the sluggish waters of swamps, oxbows, or river backwaters. They have a preference for clear water with abundant vegetation but are tolerant of silt, mud, and high temperatures. Whereas most fishes use their gas bladders for buoyancy, the bowfin can use its also to inhale atmospheric oxygen. When dissolved oxygen in the water is reduced by high temperature or decomposition, bowfins can rise to the surface and gulp air, supplementing the oxygen obtained by the gills. This adaptation helps the bowfin survive in waters where most other fish cannot. The bowfin's exceptional tenacity for life was once demonstrated to floodplain farmers of the lower Mississippi Valley, who occasionally turned up live bowfins with the plow after floodwaters had receded from farmland!

A voracious predator, the bowfin feeds principally on fish and is frequently cursed as being a greedy and amoral scourge to sport fishes. Bowfins are also portrayed as "bad guys" because they compete with more palatable sport fishes for food and take any bait or lure that the bass- or catfisherman has to offer. As any grinnel fisherman can tell you, the bowfin takes bait with a tremendous rush and is extraordinarily strong on the hook—a game opponent for any angler with a healthy heart, a stout rod, and leather gloves (watch out for its teeth!). The bowfin is known colloquially as cottonfish, for when improperly cooked or eaten cold the flesh is said to ball up in one's mouth like cotton. Epicures have recently given rave reviews, however, to "Cajun caviar," a delicacy made from the roe of the choupiquet. The bowfin has also been ascribed the peculiar denomination of John A. Grindle after an eighteenth-century Indiana lawyer who was fond of fishing.

In late spring, the male bowfin roots a

shallow nest into a weedy swamp or slough bottom; after the eggs are deposited and fertilized, he guards the nest and fry until the young fish can fend for themselves.

Young bowfins make interesting pets and are well behaved in an aquarium, provided of course that one does not trust them with smaller fish.

Freshwater Eels

Family ANGUILLIDAE

The eels come from what we call the entrails of the earth. These are found where there is much rotting matter, such as in the sea, where seaweeds accumulate, and in the rivers, at the water's edge, for there, as the sun's heat develops, it induces putrefaction.
—Aristotle

American Eel

Anguilla rostrata

Plate 13

Colloquial names: snakefish, freshwater eel

Scientific name:
Anguilla, Latin for "eel"
rostrata, Latin for "beaked," in reference to the snout

Distribution: Along the Atlantic and Gulf coasts of North America, moving inland in large rivers. In our region, occurring throughout much of the Mississippi drainage from South Dakota and southern Minnesota to eastern New Mexico and Texas.

Size: Up to 1–3 feet long and 6 pounds. The official world record is 8 lbs. and was taken in Long Pond, New York, in 1987.

Status: Dams preventing upstream migration have reduced their abundance in some states; of limited value as a sport fish.

The eel is unique among North American fishes because of its unusual catadromous life cycle. In contrast to the anadromous salmon, eels spawn in the ocean, supposedly at a depth of 1500 feet or more in the Sargasso Sea near Bermuda. The transparent young drift on ocean currents to the coasts of North and South America; from there the females continue the migration into rivers, including the Mississippi River and its tributaries in the central United States. The immature eels, called elvers, develop as adults in coastal or inland waters before returning to the sea to spawn and die. The male eel normally stays in the brackish water of the estuary. Thus, any eel taken inland is most assuredly a female.

The location of the eel's spawning ground remained a mystery to science until 1922, when the Danish oceanographer and biologist Johannes Schmidt announced the discovery of the spawning ground for the European eel. Schmidt and his associates had collected leptocephali (eel larvae) since 1904 by trawling in waters of the Atlantic ocean. By collecting larvae in increasingly younger stages of development, Schmidt eventually traced the spawning ground across the Atlantic Ocean to the vicinity of the Sargasso Sea. Both the American and European eels are thought to breed in or near the Sargasso Sea.

Eels seem to prefer live food and generally feed at night on aquatic invertebrates and fish. Eels can be caught at night with rod and reel, or they can be speared as they lie buried in the mud during the day. Once captured, they should be handled with leather gloves, because they are indeed as "slippery as an eel" and will bite. Eels are also taken commercially, with much of the catch being exported to Europe. Although the eel is not commonly thought of as a food fish in our region, smoked eel is considered a real delicacy.

Herrings

Family CLUPEIDAE

Between dark hills on either side
The salt sea-loch runs for a mile,
And now, sun-charmed to a smile,
Gleams bright its flowing frothing tide.
But lo! each wave to silver turns
In dazzling fire the whole loch burns,
Millions of Herring dart and splash
Each one a living lightning flash.
—William Sharp
  A Herring Shoal

The herrings are principally a marine family with a worldwide distribution; the family includes such species as the menhadens and sardines. Some species of herrings will wander short distances into fresh water, and four species are established in inland waters of North America. The freshwater herrings are bright, silvery, slab-sided fishes that live near the water's surface, where their shape and color pattern make them difficult to see from below. The alewife and the shads typically feed on plankton and are important forage species, although they sometimes overpopulate lakes. The skipjack, our only carnivorous herring, feeds on small fish.

Herrings have several modifications that set them apart from most other fishes. A herring's belly has a sharp, "sawtoothed" edge, formed by a row of specially modified scales. Herrings also have a transparent "eyelid" that covers each eye, with a vertical, football-shaped slit exposing the pupil.

Herrings are one of the most important families of food fishes in the world, and much of the commercial catch is processed into fish meal, a major source of protein in livestock feed and pet food. Two of our common freshwater herrings, the threadfin and gizzard shads, are among the most widely stocked forage fishes in the United States. Herrings are fragile fishes, and they usually die once they are taken from the water or otherwise handled—hence the common phrase "dead as a herring."

Alewife

Alosa pseudoharengus

Plate 17

Colloquial names: ellwife, sawbelly, golden shad, branch herring, river herring, spring herring, gaspereau

Scientific name:
Alosa, old Saxon name *allis* for the European shad
pseudoharengus, Greek for "false herring"

Distribution:
Along the east coast of North America. Landlocked in many northern lakes, including the Great Lakes. Introduced into Merritt Reservoir in Nebraska.

Size: About 5–7 inches in freshwater; anadromous specimens to 14 inches.

Status: Not threatened in any state.

The alewife is a schooling fish with bright silvery and iridescent sides. Landlocked populations inhabit all depths of open lake waters during most times of the year but avoid deep, extremely cold waters. Alewives feed principally on zooplankton and have been introduced into some water-supply reservoirs in the eastern United States in an attempt to control plankton blooms, in lieu of chemical control with copper sulfate.

Coastal populations of the alewife are anadromous (moving up streams to spawn), whereas landlocked alewives are content to spawn near lake shores in wave-swept shallows or other moving water. Spawning takes place at night, when alewives scatter their eggs over sand or gravel bottoms. Inland alewives mature at a younger age than Atlantic alewives and do not grow as large as their seagoing brethren. After the sea lamprey nearly eliminated the chief predators of the alewife (lake trout and burbot) in Lake Michigan during the 1940s and 1950s, the alewife populations exploded and the species made up the bulk of fish weight in the lake. In the 1960s, health risks were posed by the massive numbers of alewives that washed ashore during the species' annual die-offs in the Great Lakes. The exact cause of these die-offs is unknown but is thought to be related to seasonal temperature changes in the water. In the 1960s, the coho salmon was introduced successfully into Lake Michigan to help control the alewife population.

Inland alewives are an important forage species, especially for salmon and trout, and many alewives are harvested for fish meal destined for poultry farms. The larger alewives from the coast are also used for human consumption.

Skipjack Herring

Alosa chrysochloris

Plate 14

Colloquial names: blue herring, golden shad, river shad, river herring, nailrod, skippy

Scientific name:
Alosa, old Saxon name *allis* for the European herring
chrysochloris, Latin for "golden-green," a reference to the color of the back

Distribution: Mississippi River and other Gulf Coast drainages from Texas to Florida.

Size: Commonly 12–16 inches to a maximum of about 21 inches. The world record is 3 lbs. 12 oz., caught in 1982 from Watts Bar Lake in Tennessee.

Status: Protected in Iowa and of special concern in South Dakota.

The skipjack herring prefers the moderately clear, deep waters of large rivers and often congregates in the swift currents below dams. The skipjack is also common in the brackish waters of the Gulf Coast, where it commonly enters the major rivers. In the Mississippi River system, the skipjack's abundance has been affected by river modifications. Dams on the upper Missouri River and dredging of the lower Missouri have reduced the turbidity, stabilized the flow, and deepened the channel, producing favorable conditions for skipjacks in the lower reaches of this river. Skipjacks now occur in the Missouri River as far north as the Gavins Point Dam on the Nebraska–South Dakota border. Conversely, because the skipjack is a migratory species, the many lock-and-dam structures on the Mississippi River have hindered upstream movement by skipjack herrings and have probably extirpated the species from the upper reaches of that river.

Unlike the shads and alewife, the skipjack herring is carnivorous and eats small fishes and invertebrates. The skipjack herring will frequently "skip" over the water's surface in pursuit of prey; its lightning speed and camouflage coloration make it nearly impossible to follow with the naked eye. Little is known about the spawning habits of this species, but some researchers suspect the species to be anadromous.

Skipjack herrings can be caught on hook-and-line with minnows or spinners as bait. Although not highly regarded as food, the skipjack is a strong fighter when hooked. Anglers value the skipjack for catfish bait because of its scented oils and sometimes capture skipjacks below dams in dip or throw nets.

Gizzard Shad

Dorosoma cepedianum
Plate 15

Colloquial names: hickory shad, skipjack, mud shad, sawbelly, flatfish, stink shad (for their peculiar odor when fresh)

Scientific name:
Dorosoma, Greek for "lance-body," the shape of the larvae
cepedianum, for Cityon Lacépède, a French naturalist who first described several species of fishes found in North America in his *Histoire Naturelle des Poissons* (Natural History of the Fishes)

Distribution: Native to the eastern United States but widely stocked throughout the states as a forage fish in ponds and reservoirs.

Size: Commonly 9–15 inches, up to about 24 inches. The North American record of 4 lbs. 5 oz. was caught in the St. Clair River, Ontario, on February 18, 1985.

Status: Not threatened in any state.

The gizzard shad is the most widely distributed species of herring in the United States. A native of sluggish, low gradient streams, the gizzard shad has been introduced widely and successfully as a forage fish into reservoirs across the United States. The gizzard shad has a deep body profile but like other herrings is laterally compressed and "flat as a pancake." Young shad travel in schools, often near the water's surface, sometimes jumping clear of the water or gliding across the surface on their sides in attempts to escape predators. We have often had gizzard shad escape our seines by skittering across the surface on their sides, only to frantically jump back into our nets from behind.

Gizzard shad eat plankton and other floating organisms, and schools are often seen in shallow water gleaning algae from rocks. This species will occasionally ingest sand, apparently to aid digestion in its muscular gizzard—hence the common name. According to George Browne Goode in his book *American Fishes,* the colloquial name hickory shad also refers to the gizzard, "which is about the size of a hickory-nut." The flesh and gizzard of the species are commonly fermented for catfish "stink" bait.

The gizzard shad is extremely prolific and can deposit as many as 400,000 eggs. In warm, shallow lakes, especially those of moderately high turbidity, shad can become a nuisance. The adult shad may grow too quickly and become too large for use as forage and will compete with other fishes for space and food (the young of some sport fishes also consume plankton).

Threadfin Shad

Dorosoma petenense

Plate 16

Colloquial names: shad, yellowfin shad

Scientific name:
Dorosoma, Greek for "lance-body," in reference to the larvae
petenense, Latinization for "from Peten," a reference to Lake Peten, Yucatan, the type locality where this species was first described.

Distribution: Mississippi and other Gulf Coast drainages from Florida to Central America. Widely introduced into reservoirs in the southern United States.

Size: Usually 4–6 inches, up to about 9 inches maximum.

Status: Stocked as a forage fish. Not threatened.

The threadfin shad is similar to the gizzard shad in appearance and habits. It inhabits lakes, reservoirs, and large rivers, where it is sometimes found in swifter water than its congeneric relative. Threadfin shad are not as tolerant of cold water as gizzard shad (die-offs can occur at 45°F), so their distribution is limited to the southern United States. Like the gizzard shad, threadfins travel in large schools near the water's surface, eating plankton that they filter from the water. Spawning occurs in shallow water as threadfins charge the shorelines or riverbanks, occasionally becoming so excited that they beach themselves. The eggs are adhesive and attach to the lake or river bottom.

Threadfin shad have been stocked as a forage fish in many reservoirs in the southern United States, and in this capacity have some advantages over gizzard shad. Threadfins have only about half the lifespan of the gizzard shad and grow only about half as big, staying within a size range that is exploitable by sport fishes. Because of the limited tolerance of threadfin shad to cold water temperatures, they probably cannot be stocked with much success north of Oklahoma or central Missouri.

Mooneyes

Family HIODONTIDAE

They will come up, taste of a fly, let go and be
gone before the angler has time to strike.
Therefore, to be a Moon-eye fly-fisher one must
be very sharp and not read a book while
casting, as I once knew a man to do.
—Dr. D.C. Estes,
  quoted in American Fishes

Mooneye and Goldeye

Hiodon tergisus and *Hiodon alosoides*

Plates 18–19

Colloquial names: Mooneye-toothed herring, freshwater herring, white shad Goldeye-yellow herring, northern mooneye, la quesche

Scientific name:
Hiodon, Greek for "toothed hyoid," a reference to the bone forming the base of the tongue
tergisus, Greek for "polished," possibly a reference to the sheen of the body
alosoides, from the Latin and Greek meaning "shadlike"

Distribution: The goldeye occurs across Canada and much of the Mississippi drainage, from western Montana to the Gulf of Mexico, but is uncommon or absent over most of the High Plains except along the Missouri River. The mooneye occurs in the Mississippi River and its larger tributaries, the Great Lakes (excepting Superior), and the Red River of North Dakota and Minnesota.

Size: The goldeye reaches 15 inches and 2 pounds. The world record of 3 lbs. 13 oz. came from the Lake Oahe tailwaters in South Dakota in 1987. The mooneye grows to about 12 inches, and the world record weighed 1 lb. 7 oz.

Status: The goldeye is protected or of special concern in Wyoming, Wisconsin, and Mississippi. The mooneye is of special concern in South Dakota and several other states.

The goldeye and mooneye are endemic to the United States and Canada and are the only members of the Hiodont family. The species resemble shads or herrings but can be distinguished by the posterior placement of the dorsal fin and the numerous small teeth on their jaws, mouths, and tongues. The large eyes of the mooneye and goldeye are well adapted to turbid waters and the species' nocturnal habits. The goldeye gets its common name from the bright golden color of its iris, whereas the iris of the mooneye is a lighter shade of gold or silver, resembling the coloration of a "full moon."

Goldeyes and mooneyes both inhabit large rivers and lakes, but each prefers different types of water. The goldeye inhabits the quiet, turbid waters of river pools and muddy shallows of lakes, and the mooneye has a preference for moving waters and clearer, less silted habitats. Both species typically move upstream to spawn although the goldeye is also known to spawn in shallow areas of some lakes. No nests are built. The eggs of the goldeye are semibuoyant and develop as they drift in the water.

As their impressive array of teeth would indicate, goldeyes and mooneyes are strict predators that feed near the water's surface. Their principal sources of nourishment are insects, invertebrates, small fish, and even a hapless mouse or two. Both the goldeye and mooneye will readily take a fly, lure, or baited hook, and goldeyes are sometimes caught when deep trolling for salmon or trout.

Goldeyes are taken commercially and are considered a delicacy in Canada. Scott and Crossman, in *Freshwater Fishes of Canada,* relate an interesting story of "Winnipeg goldeye," a dish popularized on transcontinental trains in Canada. Winnipeg goldeye was originally smoked over a willow fire, which gave the skin a red to orange tint. Goldeyes are now smoked over oak fires and the skin colored with a dye to maintain the marketing image of the food product.

Salmons, Trouts, and Whitefishes

Family SALMONIDAE

Salmon, trout, carp, etc.
—Rev. J. G. Wood
  A chapter in his nineteenth-century
  Animate Creation

The auspicious chronicle of the Salmonids began in ancient Gaul when Caesar's soldiers are supposed to have applied the name of *Salmo* (from *salire,* meaning "to jump") to migrating schools of leaping Atlantic salmon. Today, the salmonids are extensively stocked and fished throughout North America and the world. In terms of dollars they are probably our most important family of fishes, considering the commercial harvests of Pacific salmons, the ocean and inland salmon fishing charters, commercial trout farming, and the economic impact of fly-fishing purists. The angler's phenomenon of "trout fever" is due as much to the sparkling, pristine habitats of the trouts as to the beauty and gameness of the fishes themselves.

Many of the salmons and trouts are anadromous fishes; that is, they live their lives in salt water and return to freshwater rivers in spectacular migrations to spawn. The salmonids have a remarkable homing ability, led by an acute sense of smell that enables them to return and spawn in the same stream in which they were hatched. After the long, arduous migration and spawn, most salmon inevitably die; but death is probably more a result of innate physiological changes than of exhaustion or injuries caused by the hardship of the journey.

The females of most salmonids use their tails to sweep nests (also called redds) into the gravel bottoms of streams. Fertilized eggs vary as to hatching times, but most take two or three months to hatch. The young of many species of salmon and trout have a series of lateral blotches termed *parr marks*, and these young are thus known as *parrs*.

Salmonids are usually found in cold, clean waters (maximum temperatures generally less than 75°F), a requirement based partially upon their need for high amounts of dissolved oxygen. Warm water holds less oxygen than an equivalent amount of cold water, so hot summer temperatures usually portend doom for put-and-take trout in shallow warm-water lakes.

The brook trout is the only salmonid native to our region outside of the Great Lakes, originally being restricted to cold-water streams in the northeast of Iowa and in southeastern Minnesota. Several subspecies of cutthroat trout are native to waters east of the Continental Divide but were originally restricted to mountain streams. The Black Hills of South Dakota have been intensively stocked with brook trout, rainbow trout, and brown trout and offer some of the better trout fishing in the Great Plains.

Chinook Salmon

Oncorhynchus tshawytscha

Plate 21

Colloquial names: king salmon, spring salmon, tyee

Scientific name:
Oncorhynchus, Greek for "hooked snout"
tshawytscha, the old Alaskan and Kamchatkan vernacular for this species

Distribution: Along the coast of North America from northern California to the Yukon River in Alaska; also along the Kamchatkan coast in Asia. Introduced into the Great Lakes and the Missouri River reservoirs in the Dakotas.

Size: The largest of the salmon, landlocked specimens frequently reaching 20 pounds. The largest known specimen was taken commercially near Petersburg, Alaska, and weighed 126 pounds. The landlocked record is 44 lbs. 9 oz. from the Credit River in Ontario in 1985. The largest sea-run salmon on sport tackle weighed 97 lbs. 4 oz.

Status: Protected spring through fall in Idaho.

The chinook well befits its title of king salmon. It is known to reach weights of 100 pounds, although most seagoing chinooks are less than 30 pounds, and most landlocked specimens less than 20 pounds. In our region, an excellent sport fishery for chinook has recently been developed on Lake Oahe, South Dakota, where anglers use the conventional downriggers and dodgers with hair flies as lures.

The chinook is sometimes confused with the coho salmon but has a longer anal fin, black gums, and a profusely spotted tail. The chinook has much the same native range as the coho, but the chinook spawns in the fall, winter, or spring (depending on the specific race) and usually ranges farther upstream into the Yukon and Columbia rivers. Like other Pacific salmons, chinook do not feed during their spawning runs, but they will strike lures and consequently provide much sport to anglers. Chinook will generally spawn and die after their fourth year of life, but a few will postpone the spawning until their fifth, sixth, or seventh year. Like the coho, the chinook seldom spawns successfully in our region, and any fishery must be maintained by stocking. The chinook is generally favored over the coho as a freshwater sport fish, because it lives four years instead of three, grows faster, and attains trophy size.

The specific epithet of *tshawytscha* substantiates any claim the chinook has to the title of "tongue-twister salmon." *Tshawytscha* and all other trivial names of the Pacific salmons (genus *Oncorhynchus*) are old Russian names for the various species. The German naturalist Wilhelm Stellar is credited with the scientific discoveries of the salmons during Dane Vitus Bering's explorations along the Kamchatkan Peninsula during the 1740s. But it was not until 1792 that German ichthyologist Johann Walbaum described the Pacific salmon, applying the Russian names that Stellar had recorded in his field notes. So how does one pronounce *tshawytscha?* We think the solution is best relegated to the name of the Pacific Indian tribe that so effectively utilized the species—Chinook!

Coho Salmon

Oncorhynchus kisutch

Plate 22

Colloquial names: silver salmon, medium red salmon (canned under this name), hooknose

Scientific name:
Oncorhynchus, Greek for "hooked snout" *kisutch,* an old Alaskan and Kamchatkan name for this species

Distribution: Along the west coast from San Francisco to the Yukon Delta of Alaska and along the Asiatic coast as far south as Japan. Introduced into the Great Lakes and Wyoming; formerly stocked into Dakota and Nebraska reservoirs.

Size: Attaining a maximum weight of 25 pounds, although most landlocked specimens weigh less than 5 pounds. The world record landlocked coho weighed 14 lbs. and was caught in Bronte Creek, Ontario, in 1988.

Status: Not protected in any state.

The coho, a member of the Pacific salmon tribe, has been successfully introduced into the Great Lakes and was formerly stocked into reservoirs of the upper Missouri River in the Dakotas. The original distribution of the coho included the west coast of North America from San Francisco to the Yukon Delta in the Norton Sound of Alaska.

Though not the largest of the salmons, the coho is considered one of the most spectacular on hook and line. Its acrobatic leaps and long, tireless runs make it an exciting quarry. Freshwater anglers fish for coho in rivers during the spawning runs or in freshwater lakes, using much the same equipment that takes lake trout. In the Great Lakes, coho typically occur in shallower waters (20–100 feet) than either the chinook or lake trout.

Coho spawn in the fall, generally in their third year of life, by migrating from the lake or ocean into their "home streams." Most strains of coho do not undertake the long and grueling migrations of the chinook and some other Pacific salmon. Accordingly, the coho is sometimes called "creekfish" for its habit of spawning in small tributary streams. This phenomenon, coupled with the species' short migrations, lets the coho avoid most of the migration problems associated with irrigation and hydroelectric dams. The male coho develops an exaggerated kype or "hook" on the upper jaw during the spawning season and is sometimes known as hooknose. The coho is particularly aggressive during the spawn, and as in other salmons, much of the bodily damage thought to be inflicted during the spawning run actually occurs during fights around the nests. Coho spawn once and die soon afterward.

In our region, the coho is likely to be confused only with the chinook salmon. The coho can be distinguished by its white gumline and by the lack of spots on the lower half of the tail (sometimes the entire tail is spotless).

Rainbow Trout

Oncorhynchus mykiss

Plate 24

Colloquial names: steelhead, kamloops, salmon trout, coast range trout, hardhead, redband

Scientific names:
Oncorhynchus, Greek for "hooked snout"
mykiss, an old Alaskan and Kamchatkan name for this species

Distribution: Native to northern Pacific drainages of North America and Asia. Stocked into many cold-water streams and into many reservoirs and their "tailwaters" in the central United States.

Size: Maximum documented weight is 52.5 pounds. Generally growing to a maximum of 10–15 pounds, although most specimens, especially in streams, are much smaller. The world record for landlocked rainbow trout is 27 lbs. 3 oz., taken from the Ganaraska River in Ontario, Canada, in May 1984.

Status: A few native strains are protected in the northwestern United States.

Worldwide, more effort may have been expended in propagation and transplantation of the rainbow trout than of any other sport fish. Originally restricted to the Pacific coasts of North America and Asia, the rainbow is now established in Hawaii, Europe, South America, New Zealand, Nepal, New Guinea, South Africa, and even Madagascar. Lake McConaughy on the North Platte River in Nebraska is the only reservoir in the Great Plains that supports a self-sustaining population of rainbow trout.

Most states in our region operate rainbow trout fisheries on a put-and-take basis for at least a portion of each year.

The rainbow's utility as a stocked fish is enhanced by its tolerance of warm water. Although the species prefers cold water, under certain conditions some strains are capable of enduring waters as warm as 80–85°F, a temperature that would be lethal to brook, brown, and cutthroat trouts.

The rainbow trout is a complex of many indistinct subspecies. The better-known varieties include the kamloops trout, which is a large, pot-bellied lake rainbow indigenous to deep lakes in British Columbia. The steelhead is an anadromous rainbow native to the northwestern United States and coastal Alaska. A third "species" of rainbow trout, formerly known as *Salmo irideus,* originally occurred west of the Sierra Nevadas from the Mexican border to Oregon and completed its life cycle within fresh water.

The rainbow trout was first transplanted into the eastern states in 1880, after strains of the colorful McCloud River rainbow trout were successfully propagated by the U.S. Fish Commission on the McCloud River in California. Angling purists originally balked at the idea of having their brook trout streams "contaminated," but many became supporters of the program once they discovered the gameness and utility of the rainbow.

Efforts to establish the rainbow trout as a stream fishery in the eastern United States have met with mixed results, principally because rainbow trout tend to emigrate downstream into lakes or reservoirs.

Cutthroat Trout

Oncorhynchus clarki

Plate 23

Colloquial names: blackspotted trout, native trout, mountain trout (Rio Grande, Lahontan, Snake River, Colorado, Yellowstone, and coastal cutthroats are a few of the well-known subspecies)

Scientific name:
Oncorhynchus, Greek for "hooked snout" *clarki*, named for Captain William Clark of Lewis and Clark fame

Distribution: Native to the Rocky Mountains and the Pacific coast from southern California to Alaska. The Yellowstone cutthroat is native to mountain headwaters of the upper Missouri drainage, and the greenback cutthroat is known from the upper South Platte and Arkansas drainages. Within our region, the cutthroat is known from a few stocks planted in Arkansas and South Dakota.

Size: Commonly 10–15 inches long in streams. Lake and anadromous strains grow to 5 pounds or more. The world record cutthroat was the Lahontan subspecies and weighed an impressive 41 lbs., caught in Pyramid Lake, Nevada, in December 1925.

Status: Several subspecies are protected in the western United States.

The cutthroat trout is a complex entity comprised of a plethora of subspecies, each distinct with regard to color and locality. The variations were brought about through geologic time and natural isolation of populations in lakes and river headwaters throughout the mountainous, arid west. Thus, many forms of the cutthroat were indigenous to one body of water, as their old vernacular names suggest: silver trout of Lake Tahoe, Waha-Lake trout, longheaded trout of Crescent Lake, and so on.

The original range of most cutthroat subspecies has been greatly reduced because of stream degradation and competition with introduced trouts. Hybridization with the rainbow trout, which has been introduced into many cutthroat waters, has placed some cutthroat subspecies in danger of extinction. Thus, cutthroat strains have lost much of their "gene pool integrity" through hybridization, and the purebred strains are now restricted to hatcheries and some high mountain headwaters.

Within our region, the Snake River cutthroat has been stocked in Arkansas and in the Black Hills of South Dakota. The greenback cutthroat, *Oncorhynchus clarki stomias*, which is restricted to the frigid waters of the South Platte and upper Arkansas rivers in Colorado, was once described as being indigenous to the warm and turbid waters of the Great Plains. "The Kansas River Trout," as George Goode called the species in his *American Fishes*, was supposedly "distributed from the Kansas River to the Upper Missouri," a statement undoubtedly based on a mixup of localities.

Because of its frequent hybridization and many color variations, the cutthroat is sometimes difficult to recognize. The majority of cutthroats, however, have (as do some hybrids) a yellow-orange to red "slash" just below the lower jaw or dentary bone. The species was originally known as blackspotted trout, a name that still holds favor with some old-time anglers. Nineteenth-century writer Charles Hallock was one of the first to propose the name of "cutthroat trout," which ichthyologist Goode termed a "horrible name," one he hoped would "never be sanctioned in litera-ture." He had, perhaps, a tenable point, for the phrase "catching a Snake River cut-throat" is somewhat reminiscent of a "B run" western movie and its black-hatted gang of renegades.

Brown Trout

Salmo trutta

Plate 25

Colloquial names: German brown trout, European brown trout, Von Behr's trout, Loch Leven trout, liberty trout (a name established during World War I in avoidance of the widespread term German brown)

Scientific name:
Salmo, Latin for "Atlantic salmon"
trutta, Latin for "trout"

Distribution: A native of Europe. Several of the 16 European subspecies have been introduced into many cold-water streams and lakes across North America. Most abundant in our region in northeast Iowa, in the Black Hills of South Dakota, and in the upper White River of northern Arkansas.

Size: Usually less than 10 pounds, but lake specimens might grow to 30 pounds. Most specimens from heavily fished streams weigh less than 1 pound. The world record brown trout weighed 38 lbs. 9 oz. and was caught in the North Fork of the White River of Arkansas in 1988.

Status: Introduced sport fish.

The brown trout began a transatlantic odyssey in February 1883 when eggs shipped by Herr Von Behr, the president of the Deutsche Fischerie-Verein, arrived in New York to the consignment of a conservationist named Fred Mather. Over the course of the next several years Mather received more shipments from Von Behr, including eggs of the Loch Leven brown trout from Scotland, which he distributed, propagated, and successfully transplanted into American waters.

The introduction of the brown trout was widely assailed by American anglers, who thought the species a fat, coarse, "weed" of a trout that would foul the pristine habitats of the native brook trout. But as anglers became more familiar with the brownie, the species became a popular sport fish. The brown trout's wily disposition, larger average size, and pugnacious character make it more attractive to some anglers than either the rainbow or brook trouts. A portion of the brown trout's rise to prominence is due to its tolerance of warmer and slightly polluted waters, which has enabled the species to spread outside of the range of the brook trout.

The brown trout can be recognized by its combination of black and orange spots. The male is more brightly colored than the female and takes on a brilliant golden hue during the breeding season. Specimens from lakes are sometimes silvery in color like the salmons but retain the characteristic spotting of the species.

Brook Trout

Salvelinus fontinalis

Plate 26

Colloquial names: speckled trout, specks, eastern brook trout, squaretail, brookie, char, whitefin, native trout

Scientific name:
Salvelinus, an old name for char, derived from the same root as *saibling,* the German word for "little salmon"
fontinalis, Latin for "living in springs"

Distribution: Introduced throughout North America and Europe and in many of our states, including Arkansas and the Black Hills of South Dakota. Native populations in Minnesota and northeast Iowa.

Size: Generally less than 1 pound, although 2- and 3-pound fish were common in the nineteenth century. The typical hook-and-line specimen is probably less than 10 inches. The world record brookie weighed 14 lbs. 8 oz. and was caught from the Nipigon River in Ontario in 1916.

Status: Native populations of some concern in New Jersey and Tennessee.

More so than any other salmonid, the brook trout is responsible for the popularity of the American trout fishery. It was the brook trout that pioneered American pisciculture in 1853; the brookie, whose cunning and spirited battles became the very heart and soul of the early American flyfishers and whose graceful, colorful contour is synonymous with the cold, clear waters of the unspoiled backcountry.

The native range of the brook trout included the Great Lakes region, north into Manitoba and eastward to Labrador, and southward into the high mountain waters of the Georgia Appalachians. The brook trout is intolerant of pollution, silt, and warm water, and wherever the brookie is found, one can be assured that its habitat is largely undisturbed. During the nineteenth and early twentieth centuries, the brook trout vanished from much of its original range as a consequence of pollution and expansive logging.

The brook trout is a handsome species and is typically cloaked in hues of rich olive-brown, but its colors may range from iridescent silver to coal black. Males exhibit the hooked upper jaw characteristic of salmonids during breeding, and their bellies blush with a brilliant orange or crimson.

The brook trout was first described in 1814, when it received the scientifically poetic denomination of *Salmo fontinalis.* When the species was excised from the genus *Salmo* and reassigned to *Salvelinus* in the late 1800s, some protest was stirred among anglers, culminating in a rhetorical discontent from Charles Hallock as published in the *American Angler.* Beginning with the assertion "I am *Salmo fontinalis,*" Hallock concludes his derision of scientific America thus:

No fulsome titles do I covet,
 Science holds no bribe for me.
Slavery for those who love it.
From nomenclature leave me free,
 Yet they call me *Salvelinus,*
 Can you fancy sin more heinous?

Lake Trout

Salvelinus namaycush

Plate 27

Colloquial names: mackinaw, laker, Great Lakes trout, gray trout

Scientific name:
Salvelinus, an old name for char, derived from the same root as *saibling*, the German word for salmon
namaycush, an Indian name meaning "tyrant of the lakes"

Distribution: From Alaska eastward across Canada, south into British Columbia, northern New England, and the Great Lakes. Introduced into the central Rocky Mountains, Arkansas, the Dakotas, and Switzerland and Denmark in Europe.

Size: Attained weights of 40 pounds in the nineteenth century, to a maximum of about 100 pounds. Today, the typical specimen weighs less than 10 pounds. The world record on hook-and-line is 65 pounds, caught in 1970 from Great Bear Lake in the Northwest Territory of Canada.

Status: Presently not listed as threatened or endangered in any state.

The lake trout is the prodigious member of the salmonid group known as chars. In lieu of more technical features, chars can be recognized by their light-colored spots on a dark background, in contrast to the dark spotting of most other salmonids. The lake trout is a close kin of the brook trout, with which it is sometimes hybridized in hatcheries, producing the "splake" (the *sp* being derived from speckled trout, the Canadian vernacular for brook trout).

The lake trout is just what its name implies, an inhabitant of deep, oligotrophic lakes. The laker's penchant for cold water pushes it to depths of 200–300 feet during the heat of summer, but from late fall through spring, lake trout sometimes emerge from the "abyss" to feed in shallows. Lake trout are fall spawners but do not build nests. Instead, females deposit their eggs over shoals or rock reefs, where crevices serve to hide the eggs from predators.

The Great Lakes were nearly depleted of lake trout in the middle portion of this century after the parasitic sea lamprey invaded the upper lakes in the 1920s via the Welland Ship Canal and Lake Erie. In the 1950s, larvicides specific to lamprey were developed and applied to the rivers and streams where the sea lamprey was known to breed, and the species has since been brought under control. The host lake trout have recovered with the aid of an intensive stocking program and are again providing a sport fishery. Lake trout plantings aim to reestablish natural spawning in the Great Lakes.

Lake trout in our region have been stocked in Arkansas and the Dakotas in the Missouri Reservoir System. Anglers usually troll for lakers in deep water by dragging or bouncing their downrigger sets in sandbars and rocks, a technique that stirs up the bottom fauna and attracts hungry lake trout.

Lake Whitefish

Coregonus clupeaformis
Plate 20

Colloquial names: whitefish, common whitefish, humpback whitefish, Great Lakes whitefish

Scientific name:
Coregonus, Greek for "angled pupil of the eye"
clupeaformis, Latin for "shad-shape"

Distribution: Throughout the Great Lakes and most of Canada. Stocked into our range in Montana and Lake Sakakawea in North Dakota and occasionally taken from Lake Oahe in South Dakota.

Size: Formerly reaching 20 pounds, commercial operations now average 2–5 pounds. The world record for hook-and-line is 15 lbs. 6 oz., taken from Clear Lake in Ontario, Canada, May 21, 1983.

Status: Protected in Illinois.

The lake whitefish is the largest and best-known member of the coregonines, a widespread and taxonomically confusing subfamily of the salmons that includes the ciscoes and the inconnu. The lake whitefish formerly supported intensive commercial fishing in the Great Lakes, but the sea lamprey, pollution, and overfishing have contributed to a sharp drop in populations of whitefish and a decline in the number of commercial fishery operations.

The whitefish is subtly colored with a beautiful pearly luster about its back and upper sides. Larger specimens develop an unappealing "hunchback" along the nape but are extremely valuable foodfish, excellent in chowders or when smoked or baked whole. Commercial fishermen generally use gill nets (as long as 600 feet) to capture whitefish, a method that unavoidably kills some sport fishes, raising objections from some charter fishing services in the Great Lakes. As a result of the fishery decline in the Great Lakes, most whitefish now marketed are from inland Canadian lakes.

The lake whitefish is a cold-water species that spends most of its time in deep waters in loosely aggregated schools. In early spring, and again during the fall spawn, lake whitefish move from deep to shoal waters and become more accessible to anglers. Over some parts of its range, the lake whitefish moves into the shallows in early summer to feed on emerging mayflies and can be caught by fly fishermen.

Smelts

Family OSMERIDAE

You ain't et, 'till you et smelt!
—An old, pithy maxim of fishermen

Rainbow Smelt

Osmerus mordax

Plate 28

Colloquial names: American smelt, ice-fish, frostfish

Scientific name:
Osmerus, Greek for "odorous"
mordax, Latin for "biting"

Distribution: Stocked into the Great Lakes watershed and rivers of the northeastern United States, originally occurring along the east coast from New Jersey to Labrador, and along the Alaskan coast. Now common in the Missouri and lower Mississippi rivers as a result of introductions into Lake Sakakawea and Lake Oahe in the Dakotas. Smelt can also access the Mississippi via the Chicago sanitary canal and the Illinois River.

Size: Commonly 6–8 inches long, to a maximum of about 13 inches.

Status: Introduced into our range.

The rainbow smelt is a slender and colorful fish that takes its name from the ancient Anglo-Saxon word *smoelt*, which means "smooth" or "shining." The name *smelt* also may have some roots in the peculiar odor of the fresh fish, which supposedly is similar to that of a cucumber.

Smelt are found principally in colder waters of the Arctic or northern latitudes. Those populations with access to the sea are anadromous (live in the ocean and move into streams to spawn), but landlocked individuals complete their life cycle in fresh water. The only species of smelt in the central United States is the rainbow smelt, which has been stocked into some large northern reservoirs and the Great Lakes. The rainbow smelt is a schooling fish that prefers the open water of lakes and will sometimes emigrate long distances both upstream and downstream from reservoir dams. Smelt are sensitive to light and stay in deeper water during the day, rising toward the surface to feed in the evening.

Landlocked smelt migrate from lakes into streams to spawn and occasionally spawn over offshore rocks in lakes. Large postspawning die-offs occur in many populations. Sexual maturity is reached in about two years, and the normal life span for rainbow smelt is eight years.

The rainbow smelt has a toothy mouth and feeds on aquatic invertebrates and small fish. The species was introduced into the Great Lakes as a forage fish and is valuable in this capacity. However, some debate has raged recently as to whether the tremendous populations of smelt could degrade commercial and sport fishing by consuming young fishes. But the rainbow smelt is an important commercial food fish in its own right. The smelt's spectacular spawning runs in tributaries of the Great Lakes herald the annual Smelt Jamborees, when millions of pounds of smelt are collected in nets, buckets, spaghetti colanders, and anything else that will strain water. In some states, smelt is the only sport fish that can legally be collected with a net. Smelt are usually eaten fried, and the gastronomist goes for bones and all!

Pikes

Family E S O C I D A E

Look at any member of the Pike family, and tell
me whether it does not make you think of a
pirate. Observe the yawning sepulchre of a
mouth, that evil eye, and low, flat forehead—
indicating a character replete with cunning and
ferocity. Note the total absence of a dignified
and respectable front dorsal fin, *which nearly*
every fish of proper moral character possesses
and displays with pride.
—*William T. Hornaday*
 The American Natural History

The pikes are a well-known and incessantly greedy group of fishes, with "eyes that are bigger than their stomachs." Their gluttony and unpredictable rapacity are legendary and afford them much popularity as sport among fishermen. As Izaak Walton presupposed: "And doubtless a pike in his height of hunger, will bite at and devour a dog that swims in a pond, and there have been examples of it, or the like; for as I told you, 'the belly has no ears when hunger comes upon it.'" The family is composed of one genus, *Esox,* and four species that are native to North America; one of these, the northern pike, is also native to Europe and Asia.

The pike family is a confusing hodge-podge of interchangeable common names. *Esox lucius,* the northern pike, might be known by any of a dozen denominations ("jack," "lance," and "pickerel" among these) that could also be applied appropriately to any other member of the family. The name *pike* came about as a reference to the fish's pointed snout and its resemblance to a "pike" or point of a lance. *Pickerel* is likewise traced to Middle English as a di-

minutive of *pike,* thus *pikerel* in its original form. At one time in England, "pickerel," "jack," "pike," and "luce" were all used to distinguish the northern pike at its various stages of growth.

Pikes are mainly fishes of clear rivers and lakes. As their sharp teeth suggest, pike are wholly carnivorous, chiefly piscivorous, and even cannibalistic! They are patient and efficient foragers that feed by ambushing prey from the concealment of weeds or rocky ledges; a single, powerful lunge is generally all that is needed to procure a meal. The exceptional voracity of the pikes makes them useful as top carnivores in the food web. Thus, northern pike and muskellunge are sometimes stocked into reservoirs with the hope that they will control populations of abundant, slow-growing panfishes.

Pikes spawn in the spring, during or soon after the breakup of ice, though pickerels will occasionally breed again in autumn if water temperatures remain high. All species of pikes spawn in shallow, decaying marshlands or weedy backwaters, where the female is usually accompanied by two or more males. The female deposits as many as 100,000 eggs into decaying vegetation, and they are simultaneously fertilized by the attending males. The eggs are then abandoned and left to develop on their own. Immediately after hatching, the young fish begin to feed on small aquatic crustaceans and within a week are devouring fish. Nature has provided an ideal avenue for young pikes to develop, for the decaying matter of the spawning ground provides both a hiding place for the young and a nutrient-rich "soup" for the tiny crustaceans that are the pike's first food. Consistent with ancient teachings, Walton suggested that pikes might also be generated from the pickerel weed: "This weed and other glutinous matter with the help of the Sun's heat in some particular months, and some ponds apted for it by nature do become pikes!"

Grass Pickerel

Esox americanus

Plate 29

Colloquial names: brook pickerel, banded pickerel, little pickerel, pond pike, trout pickerel, grass pike, mud pickerel, bulldog pickerel

Scientific name:
Esox, an old European name for "pike"
americanus, Latin for "of America"

Distribution: Eastern third of the United States. Our subspecies is found in eastern Iowa, southeast Missouri, southeast Oklahoma, Arkansas, Louisiana, and east Texas. A disjunct population occurs along the Niobrara and Loup rivers in Nebraska.

Size: Smallest of the pikes, generally less than 10 inches. The world record was a redfin subspecies weighing 2 lbs. 10 oz.

Status: A sport fish through most of its range but protected in Iowa.

Misplaced amidst the giants of the Pike family, the grass pickerel appears as a miniature replica of its toothy kin. Often mistaken for young northern pike, the grass pickerel is common in rivers and lakes and is the only member of the family that inhabits brooks and small intermittent streams. Because of its small size and smaller space requirements, the grass pickerel seems to be more gregarious than other pikes, and a dozen or more can be captured with one sweep of a seine. The eminent ichthyologist David Starr Jordan described the grass pickerel's penchant for overcrowding during its annual spawn:

> It swarms in the spring in ponds formed by the overflow of creeks. Thousands of them are destroyed yearly by the drying of such ponds. In the spring it ascends all small streams, and it is often found in temporary brooks in cornfields and other unexpected places, remote from its native water. People finding pickerel thus stranded often affirm stoutly that they "rain down."

The grass pickerel can be discerned from the northern pike and the muskellunge by its fully scaled cheek and opercle. The species comprises two distinct subspecies: the grass pickerel, *Esox americanus vermiculatus*, and the redfin pickerel, *Esox americanus americanus*. The latter is complementary in distribution to the grass pickerel and is found principally along the east coast. The grass pickerel spawns in spring in shallow, weedy water. The species is surprisingly fecund, and a 6-inch female might deposit as many as 15,000 eggs. The grass pickerel will sometimes spawn a second time if unseasonably warm weather lasts well into autumn.

Because of the "hammerhandle's" small size and sleek build, most anglers consider it no more than a youngster's fish. We have found among our many collections a 9-incher to be a trophy fish. The grass pickerel will occasionally hybridize with the chain pickerel, producing a larger specimen with strangely patterned colors.

Chain Pickerel

Esox niger

Plate 30

Colloquial names: jack, eastern pickerel, black pickerel, green pike

Scientific name:
Esox, an old European name for "pike"
niger, Latin for "dark" or "black"

Distribution: East Coast and Gulf Coast states. In our range, occurring in Louisiana, Arkansas, southeast Missouri, southeast Oklahoma, and the eastern edge of Texas. Stocked in Nebraska.

Size: Reaching 2 feet in length and 4 pounds in weight. The world record of 9 lbs. 6 oz. was caught in 1961 near Homerville, Georgia.

Status: Of special concern in Kentucky.

The chain pickerel gets its peculiar common name from the handsome network of iridescent green "chains" that stripe its sides. The species first gained notoriety during colonial times as the Federation Pike, an honor bestowed for its concatenation of thirteen united links. Thoreau so admired the fish that he immortalized it in *Walden:*

Ah, the pickerel of Walden. They possess quite a dazzling and transcendent beauty which separates them by a wide interval from the cadaverous cod and haddock whose fame is trumpeted in our streets. They are not green like the pines, nor gray like the stones, nor blue like the sky; but they have, to my eyes, if possible, yet rarer colors, like flowers and precious stones, as if they were the pearls, the animalized nuclei or crystals of the Walden water.

Both the chain and grass pickerels have fully scaled cheek and gill covers, which distinguish them from the pike and muskellunge. A young chain pickerel also has a comparably longer snout when compared with the grass pickerel and a vertical bar below the eye; the bar of the grass pickerel is angled backward.

The chain pickerel haunts clear, weedy rivers and thickly vegetated lakes, where it basks surreptitiously within a few inches of the surface, waiting to break fast on some unsuspecting fish or frog. When the weeds are too thick for the conventional angler, pickerel can be caught by "skittering." Skittering utilizes a long bamboo pole (12 feet or more) and an equal length of line. A perch belly or frog is affixed to the hook and the bait is jerked, or skittered, across the surface of the water in efforts to entice a strike. The larger pickerels, those over 4 pounds, can usually be found in 5–10 feet of water along the edges of gently sloping weedbeds. Typically, northern pike, chain pickerels, and grass pickerels are competitively exclusive in terms of occupancy and will not coexist in the same body of water. Thus, any lake that produces a good catch of chain pickerel is usually devoid of the other pikes.

Northern Pike

Esox lucius

Plate 31

Colloquial names: pike, wolf, snake, great northern pickerel, jack, jackfish, pickerel, common pike, Great Lakes pike, American pike

Scientific name:
Esox, an old European name for "pike"
lucius, an old Latin name for this species

Distribution: A cosmopolitan species in the Northern Hemisphere. In North America, occurs in Alaska, across Canada, and in much of the northeastern United States. Becoming uncommon to the south in Kansas, Missouri, Oklahoma, etc., occurring mostly where stocked in reservoirs.

Size: Commonly growing to 20 pounds and a length of 3 feet. The North American record is 46 lbs. 2 oz. The world record came from Czechoslovakia and weighed 55 lbs. 15 oz., caught in 1979. Forbes and Richardson in their *The Fishes of Illinois* cited Pennell as reporting a pike from Europe of 145 pounds, supposedly captured in 1862.

Status: Sport fish, not threatened in any state.

The legendary northern pike is as much myth as it is fish, for the pike is a collection of the extraordinary, the improbable, the impossible, and the absurd. "More lies, to put it in very plain language," wrote the naturalist Frank Buckland, "have been told about the pike than any other fish in the world, and the greater the improbability of the story, the more particularly is it sure to be quoted."

One anecdote came from the German naturalist Konrad von Gesner. Gesner remarked upon the so-called Emperor's Pike, a fish 19 feet long and weighing some 550 pounds, that was captured in the year 1497 in a pool near Hailprun, Suabia. Attached to a gill of the fish was a brass ring bearing a Greek inscription (translated, appropriately, by the Bishop of Worms)—"I am the fish that was first put into this lake by the hands of the Emperor Frederick II, on the 5th day of October, 1230." This revelation thereby claimed for the fish an age of no less than 267 years. The skeleton of the pike was supposedly preserved in the cathedral at Mannheim, Germany, but a nineteenth-century anatomist proved the skeleton to be a composite, having been lengthened to fit the story!

Pike have an insatiable appetite. The typical northern will devour one-fifth of its weight in prey every day, eating mainly fish, but consuming almost anything with scales, fur, or feathers. Consequently, a northern is a fast growing fish, at least in the southern portion of its range, and might reach a length of 20 inches within its first three years of life. Its appetite and vulgar table manners were known to Izaak Walton: "A pike will devour a fish of his own kind, that shall be bigger than his belly or throat will receive, and swallow a part of him, and let the other part be digested, and swallow that other part that was in his mouth, and so put it over by degrees . . ."

The pike is a trophy fish to most anglers and is known for its uncalculated eagerness and unabated attacks on spoons, plugs, spinners, and flies. The species is also popular among bait fishermen who troll or "still fish" for pike using 10–12 inch suckers for bait. Spearfishing for pike in shallows and through the ice was formerly a common practice, and ice fishing for the species is still a popular sport. The "ideal" ice expedition was described in 1862 by Robert Barnwell Roosevelt in his *Game Fish of the Northern States of America and British Provinces:* "This is said to be very exciting, provided a rude hut is built over the hole, and a fire is made in the hut, and provided the fisherman, seated in a comfortable chair, provided with a book, a segar [*sic*] and a glass of hot punch, has an assistant to pull out the fish."

Muskellunge

Esox masquinongy

Plates 32–33

Colloquial names: muskie, mascalonge, chatauqua, Ohio muskie, great pike, masquinonge, lunge, white pike, white pickerel, tiger, barred muskie, Allegheny River pike, Wisconsin muskie

Scientific name:
Esox, an old European name for "pike"
masquinongy, a derivative of the Ojibwa Indian word for "strong pike"

Distribution: Limited to North America. Native to the St. Lawrence River drainage of New York and Quebec, westward across Ontario and the Great Lakes region, and south into the Ohio Valley. Stocked into many reservoirs in the north central Plains.

Size: Typically 20–30 pounds, though formerly averaging much larger. The world record was 64.5 inches long, 69 lbs. 15 oz., and was caught by Art Lawton in the St. Lawrence River, on September 22, 1957.

Status: Native populations are protected in portions of Tennessee and Ohio.

The muskellunge is an ecological anomaly. Renowned and highly revered among some anglers for its size and sporting qualities, the muskie is denounced by others as an overblown, uncatchable, and gluttonous blight on sport fishing. In either vein, the muskie is habitually misunderstood, and its intriguing habits and rapacious feeding make it an interesting and integral component of the ecosystem.

Taxonomists formerly recognized three subspecies of muskellunge: The Great Lakes or spotted muskie (pictured) is most commonly stocked in the central United States; the chatauqua (barred or Ohio muskellunge) has the spots on the sides coalesced into distinct bars; the great northern muskellunge or white pike has only faintly barred or silvery blue sides. Muskies and northern pike were often misidentified in the nineteenth century, and drawings were mislabeled in many books. The muskellunge, however, always lacks scales on the lower half of its cheek, in contrast to the northern pike's fully scaled cheek.

The name *muskellunge* has a varied and confusing philology but is thought to be a derivative of the French *masque* and *allonge*, translating to "long face." The uncertainty is confounded by the dozens of spellings. One would not find more variation at a first-grade spelling bee: *maskinonge, maskenozha, mascalonge* (Canadian), and *masq'allonge* to name only a very few.

Like other members of the Pike family, the muskellunge is a voracious, marauding "lone wolf," feeding on anything from bass and perch to ducklings, muskrats, and snakes. The muskellunge is sedentary and will usually conceal itself within the cover of the same rock bank or weedbed year after year, until forced to move by hunger or a bigger muskie.

The muskellunge is a finicky eater with a bull-headed willpower but is a savage fighter and an admirable foe when finally encouraged to bite. It is said of the muskie that an angler could cast under the auspice of a westerly wind to all of Minnesota's 10,000 lakes, and perhaps entice one strike. But let the same angler go spinning for bass, and he will land two 20-pound muskies and have a third jump into his boat.

One nineteenth-century piscator, the venerable Robert Barnwell Roosevelt, did not extol the virtues of fishing for the muskellunge:

> Believe in no one who boasts of the fine flavor of the mascallonge, cook him as you will, he is nothing but a dirty, flabby, tasteless pickerel. And as for the sport . . . sleep comfortably till either a call from your oarsman or a tug on your leg rouses you to the dreary work of pulling in a worthless, unresisting log.

During the nineteenth century, muskies consistently reached 50 pounds in weight, and specimens weighing 80 pounds or more were not uncommon, with 100 pounds being the largest substantiated claim. Most of these large muskies were known from fish markets and from hearsay of commercial fishermen, who occasionally caught large muskellunge in "pound" or trawling nets.

The tiger muskie is an artificially propagated hybrid between the northern pike and the muskellunge. Some hybrids do occur naturally, but hatchery "tigers" have been stocked in some of our more southerly states. The tiger muskie retains the scaled cheek of the parent northern but has the general color pattern of the muskellunge. The world record tiger muskellunge was a 51-pound 3-ounce natural hybrid caught from Lake Vieux Desert along the Wisconsin-Michigan border in July 1919.

Mudminnows

Family UMBRIDAE

*It would be an interesting question to solve in
how little water and how compact mud this fish
can survive. Its gills present nothing peculiar in
themselves, and certainly are not powerful
enough to squeeze water out of the mud in
which we have found them buried, two (and one
four) inches deep.*
—*Charles C. Abbott*
    Fresh-Water Fishes of New Jersey

Central Mudminnow

Umbra limi

Plate 34

Colloquial names: mudfish, mudpuppy, dogfish

Scientific name:
Umbra, Latin for "shade or shadow," intended as "phantom"
limi, Latin for "mud"

Distribution: From the Great Lakes states to western Tennessee, western Iowa, and eastern South Dakota.

Size: About 2–4.5 inches.

Status: Protected or of special concern in Missouri, South Dakota, and North Dakota within the central United States.

Four species of mudminnows (in three genera) occur in North America, but only the central mudminnow inhabits the central United States. Taxonomically, the mudminnows are distant relatives of the salmons, smelts, and pikes but are unique within their group because they are adapted for life in weedy, mud-bottomed ponds, boggy lakes, and sluggish ditches. Like the bowfin and gars, mudminnows can gulp air when their waters become depleted of oxygen.

The central mudminnow is a shy, secretive fish that flees into vegetation or flocculent bottom ooze when frightened; consequently, the species is sometimes difficult to capture even where it is abundant. Mudminnows typically inhabit shallow, vegetated waters, sometimes to the exclusion of all other fishes, principally because of the high water temperatures and low oxygen associated with its stagnant habitat. Mudminnows are carnivorous and primarily feed on bottom invertebrates.

Mudminnows spawn in the spring when water temperatures and stream levels rise. The preferred spawning habitat of the central mudminnow is flooded overflow pools along the margins of streams, where the species' adhesive eggs are deposited directly on vegetation.

Hardy in the bait bucket, and long-lived on a hook, mudpuppies are often used in northern states as bait for walleye. On the periphery of its range, the central mudminnow is protected or in need of conservation.

Tetras

Family CHARACIDAE

Bait the hook well; this fish will bite!
—William Shakespeare
  Much Ado About Nothing

Mexican Tetra

Astyanax mexicanus

Plate 35

Colloquial names: banded tetra

Scientific names:
Astyanax, from Greek mythology: Astyanax was the son of the Trojan hero Hector
mexicanus, Latinized form of "Mexican"

Distribution: Northern Mexico, Rio Grande in Texas, and Pecos River in New Mexico. Introduced into Edwards Plateau of south-central Texas; also Arizona, Louisiana, and several lakes in southern Oklahoma.

Size: Up to about 4 inches.

Status: Protected in New Mexico.

The characins are a large and diverse group of fishes found in South America and Africa. Most are akin in their place in nature to the minnows of the Northern Hemisphere. The characins include the well-known piranhas of South America, but the Mexican tetra is the only native representative of the family in the United States. The tetra is native to Mexico and the lower Rio Grande and Pecos River systems of Texas and New Mexico. The species has been introduced elsewhere into the warmer waters of the south-central United States, probably as a result of its widespread use as bait. The Mexican tetra is now common in the Guadalupe River of central Texas but apparently will not survive north of Lake Texoma in southern Oklahoma. Smaller tetras do well in aquaria and are sold in pet shops.

Mexican tetras prefer streams with clear, warm water and are often found schooling in pools below runs of swift current. This aggressive fish feeds on a variety of small aquatic organisms and will occasionally attack small fish. Fortunately for swimmers, the tetra is too small to be little more than an annoyance, perhaps occasionally nipping at an exposed mole.

Minnows

Family CYPRINIDAE

Only their names and residence make one love fishes. I would know even the number of their fin-rays, and how many scales compose the lateral line. I am the wiser in respect to all knowledges, and the better qualified for all fortunes, for knowing that there is a minnow in the brook. Methinks I have need even of his sympathy, and to be his fellow in a degree.
—Henry David Thoreau
A Natural History of Massachusetts

The minnow family comprises more than 1500 species—the largest family of fishes in the world. About 250 species find their home in North America. Although most of our small fishes are minnows, all of the minnows are not small fishes. The Colorado squawfish, for instance, is a predaceous minnow of the western United States that formerly reached lengths of 5 or 6 feet, and the common carp might grow to weigh 30 or 40 pounds.

As a group, minnows live almost anywhere, eat almost anything, and exhibit almost every kind of behavior. As a result, they are a very successful family. This success is enhanced by their relatively high fecundity, with individual females producing from a few thousand to half a million or more eggs in a single breeding season! As a consequence, some species of minnows are quick to recover after oil spills or droughts have wiped out populations.

Minnows have interesting anatomical and physiological attributes, some of which are also found in other types of fishes.

Males of some species develop brilliant breeding colors that rival those of tropical fishes. In the central United States, these include the red shiner, the redbelly dace, and the cardinal shiner among others. Minnows (and a few other types of fishes) also have well-developed Weberian ossicles, a series of small bones connecting the inner ear to the swim bladder. The membranous wall of the swim bladder picks up vibrations in the water and transmits them to the ear, giving the minnows a keener sense of hearing than many other fishes. Some species of minnows, such as the shiners, transmit sounds as part of their courtship ritual; these sounds, analogous to the songs of birds, help the fish identify and communicate with members of their own species. Minnows also secrete pheromones, chemicals that are sometimes called "fright substances" because they signal danger to other minnows.

Despite general similarities among the minnows, the individual species vary greatly in their habits, their needs, and their ability to cope with environmental changes. Fathead minnows and red shiners are "pioneers" that are among the first species to invade new areas and the last to disappear as an area degrades. Others, such as the sicklefin chub and the Arkansas River shiner, are less tolerant, and their place in nature is threatened. In addition to their intrinsic and ecological values, minnows are also important around the world as bait, food, and sport fishes.

Common Carp

Cyprinus carpio
Plates 36–37

Colloquial names: German carp, European carp, scaled carp, leather carp, mirror carp, buglemouth bass, king carp

Scientific name:
Cyprinus, ancient Greek name for carp, perhaps derived from Cyprus, abode of Aphrodite (Venus), goddess of love and beauty
carpio, Latin for "carp"

Distribution: Widespread in North America south of the 50th parallel, becoming more sparsely distributed in the West.

Size: Often 1–2 feet and 1–8 pounds. The U.S. record of 57 lbs. 13 oz. was taken from the Tidal Basin, Washington, D.C., in 1983. The world record, from France, weighed 75 lbs. 12 oz.

Status: Introduced. Underutilized as a sport and food fish in the United States and Canada, where it usually is considered a nuisance species.

The common carp is one of the most well known and most persecuted warm-water fishes in the Northern Hemisphere. A native of temperate Asia, the common carp was firmly established in North America by widespread stocking in the late nineteenth century. Although initially a popular addition to the fauna of the New World, the carp quickly fell into disfavor with anglers and biologists. An overzealous stocking program combined with the carp's high fecundity and tolerance to a wide range of environmental conditions enabled it to spread throughout the United States. In some parts of their range, carp crowd native fishes and compete with them for food and other resources. Carp also stir up sediments as they root along the bottom searching for food, thereby increasing the turbidity of the water. But the carp is not the principal cause of murky waters; it is the siltation of our lakes and streams that has allowed the carp to exploit habitats where native fishes were adversely impacted.

Carp thrive in lakes or sluggish streams that are organically enriched and have a silty bottom, but they are less abundant or absent from cold, clean rivers or stream segments with swift flows. The carp is an opportunistic omnivore and bottom feeder, taking mostly invertebrates and green plant material.

Common carp spawn in the spring and summer as water temperatures rise. Just prior to spawning, carp wallow about in shallow water in large schools, later breaking into breeding groups that usually consist of one female and two or three males. These smaller groups then thrash about noisily in their spawning ritual, often moving into water so shallow that their backs are exposed above the surface. The eggs of the carp, which are adhesive, drift until they attach to submerged objects, where they hatch within a week.

Three varieties of common carp are raised at fish hatcheries in Europe and Asia and are also found in nature. The typical scaled carp is most abundant. The mirror carp has three irregular rows of enlarged scales and makes up less than 5 percent of the carp population at most sites. The leather carp, which is nearly or completely devoid of scales, is exceptionally rare in the wild.

Public opinions about the common carp in North America and Eurasia seem to be diametrically opposed. In the Soviet Union, for example, large minnows such as carp, "true" bream, and the goldfish are among the principal warm-water food fishes. Common carp are stocked into newly constructed impoundments and are managed with the same concern a hatchery biologist in the United States might bestow upon the black bass. The Soviets have a simple reason for their "madness": The carp is a native of the Soviet Union and adjacent countries and has provided their peoples an important source of protein for many centuries. The Soviets raise both the *sazan* or wild carp, and the *karp*, which is pond-bred like livestock. These commercial operations consist of a series of several ponds, each designed for different phases of producing marketable fish. In this manner, a relatively large amount of protein can be produced for human consumption. Naturalist Rachel Carson, in *Food from Home Waters: Food Fishes of the Middle West,* indicated that carp could produce over three times the yield of centrarchids when both were raised in ponds—cost-effective protein production!

The poor image of the common carp in North America is due in large part to its perceived undesirability as a sport and food fish. Because the carp's mode of feeding depends as much on odor and taste as on visual cues, the species is effectively fished with baits such as marshmallows, corn, and worms rather than the more "glamorous" lures and flies. But in our estimation, a hooked carp is as determined a fighter as most native sport fishes. Once caught, the carp's malady is in its tiny bones, fatty flesh, and "unpalatable" taste. But the discriminating gourmand overcomes these shortcomings by using the pressure cooker or the old reliable "taste-eraser" method of smoking the meat.

Goldfish

Carassius auratus
Plates 38–39

Colloquial names: Crucian carp, silver crucian carp, golden carp

Scientific name:
Carassius, Latinized vernacular names Karass or Karausche applied to European crucian carp (*Carassius carassius*)
auratus, Latin for "gilded" (overlain with gold)

Distribution: Sporadic distribution in the United States and in border areas of Canada and Mexico. Sometimes locally abundant.

Size: To a maximum of about 16 inches and 3 pounds, but usually much smaller.

Status: Introduced. Raised for use in ornamental ponds and aquaria. Sometimes raised as bait, but this use is prohibited in some areas.

The goldfish is one of the two species of fishes known as crucian carps in Europe and Asia. The silver crucian carp, which was introduced into the United States in the 1800s, is native to China and has been bred through the centuries to produce the multitude of colorful and often grotesquely shaped goldfish found in pet shops around the world. The color of escaped or "wild" goldfish is actually a dull brassy-green, which is fortunate for the goldfish because its bright orange hues would otherwise serve as a beacon to hungry predators.

Goldfish are most commonly found in impoundments and in the pools of low-gradient streams. Although some self-sustaining populations of goldfish are established in the wild, the repeated releases of unwanted pets and unused baits are usually "absorbed" through cross-breeding with established populations of common carp. Wild goldfish feed on zooplankton, aquatic insects, and plant material.

As do common carp, goldfish spawn in the spring in shallow, weedy waters. A strange phenomenon of the goldfish is the highly unusual sex ratio of the Amur subspecies in a few localities within the U.S.S.R. According to L. S. Berg in *Freshwater Fishes of the U.S.S.R. and Adjacent Countries,* the Amur male is absent or extremely rare in some lakes. The female goldfish breeds instead with males of the golden crucian carp (*Carassius carassius*) or common carp, a mating that produces only female goldfish with no inherited traits from the paternal partner! Apparently the male gamete is only needed to activate the egg and thus transfers no inheritable information.

The principal value of goldfish is as ornamental pets, and their monetary worth ranges from a few cents to several thousand dollars per fish. In Asia, the goldfish is also a relatively important food fish. In this country, goldfish are raised for bait in fish hatcheries, but the use of nonnative species for these purposes should be discouraged.

Grass Carp

Ctenopharyngodon idella

Plate 40

Colloquial names: White amur

Scientific name:
Ctenopharyngodon, Greek for "comb-like throat teeth"
idella, Greek for "distinct"

Distribution: Rivers of the lower and middle Mississippi Basin; stocked into ponds in most states.

Size: Reportedly up to 4 feet and 100 pounds in Asia.

Status: Introduced. Stocking programs controlled or prohibited in several states.

The grass carp is another of the Asian immigrants to North America, having received every bit of the fanfare of the multipurpose common carp and goldfish. A native of eastern Asia, this species is known also as the white amur for the Amur River of China and the Soviet Union. Because grass carp have a voracious appetite for aquatic vegetation, they were brought to the United States to serve as a biological control for aquatic weeds in lakes and ponds. Introduced into the United States in 1963 in Alabama and Arkansas, the grass carp was successfully spawned in 1966 and has since been distributed through much of the country by design and by accident.

Because it is a vegetarian, the grass carp is not a sport fish; but the species is a valuable source of protein in Asia. Its principal value in this country is as a control for ex-cessive growths of aquatic vegetation in lieu of chemical treatments. The control of aquatic weeds can be beneficial to anglers, especially those casting from the shore, but such vegetation also provides critical habitat to many species of sport fishes; thus, the indiscriminant use of grass carp should be discouraged.

In the wild, grass carp live in large rivers where they spawn in the more turbulent reaches of the channel, such as below a dam or at the confluence of rivers. The eggs are free-floating and will drift as far as 100 miles before hatching, whereupon the larvae find quiet, vegetated water of a marsh or backwater where they feed on zooplankton. Grass carp grow quickly after stocking, often to 10 pounds in two years. The species is long lived, and adults commonly grow to 20 pounds or more.

The grass carp's appetite for vegetation is a potential threat to rice crops and water-fowl habitat and to the spawning and feeding areas of many species of fishes. Recently, much debate has taken place as to the wisdom of bringing "another carp" to North America. Conditions for the "natural" reproduction of grass carp are thought to be limited in the United States, but some populations have reproduced, and fisheries biologists have encouraged the stocking of "sterile" populations as an added safeguard. Some state conservation agencies require permits for the distribution of the grass carp, and other states have prohibited introduction of the species.

Golden Shiner

Notemigonus crysoleucas

Plate 41

Colloquial names: American bream, American roach, shiner

Scientific Name:
Notemigonus, Greek for "angled back"
crysoleucas, Greek for "gold white"

Distribution: From the Rocky Mountains to the Atlantic Coast. Introduced into some areas of the western United States.

Size: Normally about 6 inches, to a maximum of 10–12 inches.

Status: Popular bait fish. Not threatened in any state.

Despite its name, the golden shiner does not always reflect the "Midas touch," and its colors can vary from a bright silvery luster to hues of greenish yellow or yellow brown. The golden shiner is a native of North America, but its nearest relatives are found only in Europe and Asia. Conse-quently, the species is known colloquially as bream and roach, names that are applied to some of the similar Old World minnows in England.

Golden shiners inhabit quiet, weedy areas of rivers and lakes, where they prefer clear or only slightly turbid water. The golden shiner schools in midwater or near the surface where it feeds primarily on zoo-plankton, aquatic insects, and algae. Spawning takes place near aquatic vegetation, and the adhesive eggs are left unprotected by the parents. The golden shiner is a host fish for the larva (glochidia) of the abundant and widespread "floater clam," *Anodonta grandis*, and thus helps to spread and perpetuate that species.

Large golden shiners can be caught on hook-and-line, but the principal economic value of the species is as a forage and bait fish. Most of the big shiners sold in bait shops are this species. Golden shiners are also commercially cultivated and stocked in ponds as food for sport fishes, especially largemouth bass.

Creek Chub

Semotilus atromaculatus
Plate 44

Colloquial names: horned dace, chub, mud chub, blackspot chub

Scientific name:
Semotilus, Greek *sema* means "banner" (dorsal fin), and *tilus,* as used by Rafinesque, means "spotted"
atromaculatus, Latin for "black spot"

Distribution: From the northern Great Plains to the Atlantic Coast except the Gulf Coastal Plain. Disjunct populations in northeastern New Mexico.

Size: To about 12 inches, but normally about half that length.

Status: The creek chub is not threatened in any state, but the closely related pearl dace is protected or of special concern in Iowa, Montana, Nebraska, North Dakota, South Dakota, and Wyoming.

Of the four species in the genus *Semotilus,* two are found in the Great Plains: the creek chub and the pearl dace. These fishes typically inhabit small, clear streams and are occasionally found in clear lakes. The diet of the creek chub consists chiefly of invertebrates and plant material, but adult creek chubs also eat small fish. Within the central United States, the distribution of the pearl dace is limited to the northern Great Plains; the southernmost relicts are found only in the cool, spring-fed headwaters of creeks in northern Nebraska. The creek chub is more tolerant of turbidity and can live in warmer waters than the pearl dace, which makes the creek chub the most widespread member of the genus *Semotilus.*

Creek chubs spawn over gravel bottoms in flowing water. A male fans a shallow depression into the stream bottom with his tail and removes gravel and small stones with his mouth, creating a mound of stones at the head of the spawning pit. While a female deposits eggs in the upstream end of the pit, the male elongates the pit downstream, mounding the newly excavated stones over freshly laid eggs at the head of the "trench." Continued excavation and filling of the spawning pit results in a long, low ridge. Male creek chubs are known colloquially as horned dace for the formidable tubercles that develop on their heads during the breeding season. The tubercles help the creek chub to ward off intrusions by competitors and bandits.

Creek chubs are good bait for catfishes and are easily caught on a hook. Creek chubs will provide incessant sport (or distraction) to anglers who have spent an otherwise fruitless day on the creek, and the opportunistic "chub jerker" is never "skunked." Fly fishermen are familiar with the creek chub and a northeastern species of *Semotilus,* the fallfish, both of which have the annoying habit of taking flies. Creek chubs are said to have a pleasant flavor, but like most skeptics, we have only practiced catch and release, leaving the experiments to the more enterprising epicure. Henry David Thoreau thought the flesh of the fallfish tasted like "brown paper well salted."

Redspot Chub and Hornyhead Chub

Nocomis asper and *Nocomis biguttatus*

Plates 45–46

Colloquial names: river chub, Indian chub, jerker

Scientific name:
Nocomis, an Indian name used by Charles Girard for a group of fishes
asper, Latin for "rough" (redspot chub)
biguttatus, Latin for "two-spotted" (hornyhead chub)

Distribution: Redspot chub—Ozark uplands of the Neosho-Grand drainage in Kansas, Missouri, Arkansas, and Oklahoma. Disjunct populations in the Blue River of Oklahoma and the Ouachita drainage in Arkansas.
Hornyhead chub—Generally south and west of the Great Lakes, from New York to North Dakota, with a second center of distribution in the Ozarks of Missouri and Arkansas. Isolated populations in the Platte and Cheyenne river systems of Nebraska, Colorado, and Wyoming. Not occurring with the redspot chub.

Size: Usually 5–7 inches to a maximum of about 10 inches.

Status: Both species considered of special concern in states within the central United States.

The chubs of the genus *Nocomis* are found principally in the eastern United States, but two of the seven species occur within the central United States: the hornyhead chub and the redspot chub. Both species live in clear streams with a permanent flow and a bottom of gravel or sand. Adults frequent slow runs or pools near riffles and are most at home in streams that are fringed with aquatic plants. The redspot and hornyhead chubs subsist on diets of insects and other aquatic invertebrates, occasionally ingesting some vegetation. Our two species are virtually identical in appearance, but the breeding redspot males have small tubercles on their backs and upper sides; the hornyhead male has tubercles only on its head.

Hornyhead and redspot chubs build mounded nests of gravel by carrying and depositing pebbles with their large mouths. After the spawn, the male covers the eggs with stones and actively guards the nest. Other species of minnows, such as shiners (genus *Notropis*), will sometimes spawn on *Nocomis* nests.

Large chubs are sometimes caught by anglers who are fishing for rock bass or smallmouth bass. The chubs are also used as bait, a practice that should be discouraged in areas where they are uncommon or a threatened species. The ranges of both of these species have dwindled in recent years because of increased silt loads that smother their spawning sites.

Chubs

Hybopsis spp.

Plates 42–43

Scientific name:
Hybopsis, Greek for "rounded face"

Distribution: Most species occur between the Rocky Mountains and the Appalachian Mountains, and a few are limited to the Carolinas and northern Georgia.

Size: Most species in the central United States are 2 to 4 inches long, but the flathead chub and the silver chub reach a length of 9 inches.

Status: All of the species of *Hybopsis* in the central United States are threatened or of special concern in parts of their ranges.

As are members of the genus *Nocomis,* the 18 species of the genus *Hybopsis* are properly referred to as chubs. The name *chub* is thought to derive from an old Saxon word meaning "head." Many of the European minnows known as chubs as well as the North American species of *Hybopsis* do have large heads. The name might alternatively refer to the plump body profiles of most species of chubs. All of our chubs have a small barbel or "whisker" in each corner of the mouth.

Eight *Hybopsis* chubs are found in the central United States, the flathead chub, speckled chub, and silver chub being the most widespread of our species. Some chubs reside in the quiet waters of small, clear streams, but other species inhabit the strong currents of large, turbid rivers. Whatever the stream size or turbidity level, all species of chubs prefer a clean bottom of sand or gravel. The flathead chub once inhabited all major streams of the western plains, from the Rio Grande to the Mackenzie Basin, but has since declined or disappeared where dams and irrigation diversions have reduced stream flows.

Embarrassingly little is known about the life history of the *Hybopsis* chubs, but most are thought to feed on insects and other aquatic invertebrates. Chubs have various adaptations for locating food. Those species in clear water search principally by sight, while those chubs in large, turbid rivers have well-developed external taste buds. The bigeye chub, for example, which lives in clear water and has relatively large eyes and few taste buds, is a sight-feeder. The sicklefin chub, a taste-feeder that lives almost exclusively in the turbid Missouri River, has small eyes that are partly covered with skin (to protect them from abrasion by sand) and has many taste buds over its body and in its mouth.

Because chubs require flowing water and clean sand or gravel bottoms, they have declined in abundance in the central United States, and all eight species are protected in parts of their ranges.

Authors' note: In June 1989 Dr. Richard Mayden (Univ. Kansas Mus. Nat. Hist. Misc. Publ. No. 80) proposed changes that split the genus *Hybopsis* into smaller genera.

Redbelly Daces and Finescale Dace

Phoxinus spp.

Plates 47–48

Scientific name:
Phoxinus, Greek name for an unknown river fish

Distribution: Occurring over much of the north-central United States, from the Appalachians to the Ozarks and the northern Great Plains; the northern redbelly dace also ranges northward to the Arctic. The southern redbelly dace is most common in our region in northeast Iowa, in a few streams in the Kansas Flint Hills, and in the Ozarks.

Size: Maximum length of about 2–3 inches.

Status: The northern and southern redbelly daces and the finescale dace are protected in several states within the central United States.

The five North American species of *Phoxinus* share their generic name with two European species, making them the only genus of minnows native to both the Old and New Worlds. Of the five species in North America, three occur in the central United States: finescale dace, northern redbelly dace, and southern redbelly dace.

The southern redbelly dace is most abundant in cool headwater streams in areas of groundwater seepage. Northern redbelly dace and finescale dace reside in cool bogs, lakes, and creeks, sometimes associated with beaver ponds. The latter two species frequently inhabit the same waters and hybridize freely. All of our daces seem to prefer a diet of algae but will occasionally eat aquatic invertebrates.

Two types of spawning behavior are exhibited by our daces. The males of the southern redbelly dace patiently hover in the swift water of gravel riffles, waiting for gravid females to swim into the riffle from the more tranquil water downstream. The nonadhesive eggs are deposited in the gravel and receive no parental care. The northern redbelly dace and the finescale dace mate in masses of filamentous algae. The female, with one or two males in pursuit, darts into the algal mass where the eggs are deposited. The eggs and young are not protected by the parents.

All three species can be locally abundant. They serve as food for predatory fishes and are used as bait minnows; however, where the species are uncommon near the edge of their ranges, they are sometimes protected by law. The daces are relatively docile minnows, and the male southern redbelly dace is among the most brilliantly colored of all minnows. Although the breeding males make attractive additions to an aquarium, they frequently lose their colors upon capture. The species will sometimes regain its spawning colors if the aquarium is kept cool and dark in a secluded corner.

Blacknose Dace and Longnose Dace

Rhinichthys atratulus and *Rhinichthys cataractae*

Plate 49

Colloquial names: brook minnow, black-striped minnow

Scientific name:
Rhinichthys, Greek for "snouted fish"
atratulus, Latin diminutive for "clothed in black" (blacknose dace)
cataractae, Latinized form of cataract, the original specimen being from Niagara Falls (longnose dace)

Distribution: Blacknose dace—northeastern United States and Canada, west to the eastern Dakotas and extreme northeastern Kansas.
Longnose dace—from coast to coast in Canada and the northern United States, with populations extending down the Rocky and Appalachian mountains. Also occurs in Nebraska, eastern Colorado, and the Pecos and Rio Grande drainages of New Mexico and Texas.

Size: About 2–3 inches.

Status: Neither species is protected in the central United States.

Two of the five species of *Rhinichthys* occur east of the Continental Divide: the black-nose and longnose daces. The common name of dace is a fitting title for our fishes; it originated in England as a modification of the word *darce,* meaning a "dart" or "javelin," a reference to the quick, glancing movements of minnows.

Our species of dace typically inhabit clear permanent streams, although they are occasionally found in lakes and moderately turbid streams. The longnose dace prefers swifter water, and the blacknose dace is more common in gravelly runs or pools. Both species subsist on insects and other aquatic invertebrates and small amounts of algae.

The *Rhinichthys* spawn in riffles over sand or small gravel. The male blacknose dace becomes brightly marked with yellow fins and a bright orange lateral stripe during the breeding season. The male affords no specific care to the eggs or young, but he does establish a territory and incidentally guards the eggs while defending his territory. Much of the male's time is spent bullying other males because the daces commonly eat the eggs of their own species.

The blacknose dace is a good bait minnow. Both the longnose and blacknose daces are important forage fishes, especially in trout streams.

Suckermouth Minnow

Phenacobius mirabilis

Plate 50

Scientific name:
Phenacobius, Greek for "deceptive life"
mirabilis, Latin for "wonderful" or
"strange"

Distribution: Upper Mississippi Basin
from Ohio and West Virginia through the
Dakotas and eastern Wyoming, south to
northeastern New Mexico and Alabama.
Populations also occur in other Gulf Coast
streams from the Pecos River to the Sabine
River.

Size: Usually 2–3.5 inches to a maximum
of about 4.5 inches.

Status: Endangered in New Mexico and of
special concern in South Dakota and Wyoming.

Of the five species of *Phenacobius* in North
America, only the suckermouth minnow
occurs in the central United States. The
suckermouth prefers the riffles of permanent streams with gravel or sand bottoms,
avoiding high-gradient streams and cool
waters. The species is tolerant of fluctuat-
ing water levels and turbidity, provided the
current is strong enough to keep the riffles
free of silt, and is consequently more widespread than many other "riffle" fishes. As
its ventral mouth and thick lips indicate, the
suckermouth minnow explores the sands
and gravels of the stream bottom in search
of invertebrate food. The species is thought
to spawn in late spring in riffles, but little
else is known of its spawning behavior.

The generic name of the suckermouth
minnow has an interesting derivation. As
noted, the ventral mouth, general appearance, and habits of the suckermouth are
characteristic of the bottom-feeding suckers. And according to Jordan and Evermann, in *Fishes of North and Middle America,*
"the appearance of the fish suggest[s] an
herbivorous species, which it really is not."
Hence the name *Phenacobius,* Greek for
"deceptive life."

Shiners

Notropis spp.
Plates 51–56

Scientific name:
Notropis, Greek for "back keel," a misnomer applied by Rafinesque to shriveled specimens

Distribution: From the Continental Divide to the Atlantic Coast.

Size: Most species grow to a maximum of 2–5 inches, but a few species might reach 8 inches.

Status: About a dozen species are protected in states within the central United States.

Notropis is the largest genus of fishes in North America; about 50 of the more than 100 species of *Notropis* occur in the central United States. Several species become locally abundant and are widely distributed in the Great Plains, including the red shiner, sand shiner, and emerald shiner. At the opposite extreme are several species that are considered threatened or endangered within states of the central United States. These include the Arkansas River shiner, blacknose shiner, Pecos bluntnose shiner, and Topeka shiner.

The food of shiners varies with the species and includes insects, plankton, and, for some, plant material. The mode of repro-duction also varies within the genus. Some shiners scatter their eggs; others build nests or use the nests of other kinds of fishes. An interesting example of a shiner using the nest of another fish is the association of the redfin shiner and the green sunfish described by J. R. Hunter and A. D. Hasler. Nest-building activities of the male sunfish attract the shiners; then the redfins are stimulated to spawn by the "scent" of the milt and ovarian fluid released by the sunfish. Redfin shiners have been induced to spawn in the absence of green sunfish and their nests by simply putting sunfish milt and ovarian fluid into the water. Females of some species of shiners are capable of transmitting sounds that can be detected by the males. Like the songs of birds, these sounds are species specific and help to keep the different species of shiners segregated while they spawn in the same area at the same time.

Their abundance and size make the shiners a valuable forage fish, and several of the hardier species also are used as bait. A few shiners that grow to a length of 8 inches, such as the common shiner and striped shiner, are commonly caught on hook-and-line.

Authors' note: In June 1989 Dr. Richard Mayden (Univ. Kansas Mus. Nat. Hist. Misc. Publ. No. 80) proposed changes that split the genus *Notropis* into smaller genera.

Plains Minnow

Hybognathus placitus

Plate 57

Colloquial names: gudgeon, smelt minnow, chub

Scientific name:
Hybognathus, Greek for "swollen jaw"
placitus, Greek for "a broad surface," perhaps in reference to the relatively broad snout

Distribution: In broad sandy rivers from St. Louis and the Mississippi River to central Texas, north through Montana and North Dakota.

Size: Usually 3–6 inches.

Status: The plains minnow is considered in need of conservation in Kansas. All of the species of *Hybognathus* are protected or of special concern in some parts of their ranges.

The systematics of the genus *Hybognathus* are somewhat unsettled, and the genus is generally considered to be composed of five or six species, of which three or four occur in the Great Plains: plains minnow, brassy minnow, western silvery minnow, and central silvery minnow. The latter two species are considered one and the same by some ichthyologists, who collectively term them "Mississippi silvery minnows."

As a general rule, the "Hybogs" prefer backwaters and pools of low-gradient streams where organic sediment accumulates on a sandy bottom, although the plains minnow often frequents shallow runs with moderate current. Their food consists mostly of microscopic plant and animal material gleaned from stream bottoms. Reproduction is poorly known.

The plains minnow is most common in the large, sandy rivers of the Great Plains and was formerly one of the most abundant fishes in the sandy shallows of High Plains streams. The plains minnow apparently requires strong currents of water at some stage of life, because irrigation and the subsequent "dewatering" of rivers have extirpated the species from many of its former drainages in western Kansas.

Fathead Minnow and Bluntnose Minnow

Pimephales promelas and *Pimephales notatus*
Plates 58–60

Colloquial names: Fathead minnow—blackheaded minnow

Scientific name:
Pimephales, Greek for "fathead"
promelas, Greek for "before black" (fathead minnow)
notatus, Latin for "marked or spotted" (bluntnose minnow)

Distribution: Fathead minnow—widespread from the Rocky Mountains to the Appalachian Mountains and introduced along the Pacific and Atlantic slopes. Bluntnose minnow—from the Appalachian Mountains to the eastern Great Plains from North Dakota to Oklahoma.

Size: Commonly 1.5–3.5 inches.

Status: None of the species of *Pimephales* are threatened in the central United States.

All four species of the genus *Pimephales* occur in the central United States: bluntnose minnow, bullhead minnow, fathead minnow, and slim minnow. Although they are principally riverine species (fathead minnows are commonly stocked in ponds as a forage fish), each of the *Pimephales* does best in a slightly different habitat. The fathead minnow predominates in silty pools of intermittent streams where it is tolerant of warmer temperatures and lower levels of oxygen than other species of *Pimephales*. The bluntnose minnow is most abundant in clear pools of small, permanently flowing streams. The opportunistic fathead is omnivorous and eats microscopic invertebrates, plants, and detritus. The bluntnose minnow feeds on invertebrates and algae.

Pimephales are watchful parents and staunch protectors of their eggs and young. Both the fathead and bluntnose minnows fashion nests beneath a stone, twig, or other object. The eggs are deposited in the overhanging "ceiling," and the male stands guard below them, occasionally aerating and cleaning the eggs by rubbing them with his dorsal fin and the spongy pad on his head and nape. Unwelcome visitors are apt to be "head-butted" by the male fathead, who uses the spiny tubercles on his snout to best advantage.

In its preferred habitat, the fathead minnow is often the most abundant species of fish. Fathead minnows are easy to propagate and are hardy in a bait bucket, making them one of the most commonly used bait minnows in North America.

Central Stoneroller

Campostoma anomalum

Plates 61–62

Colloquial names: greased chub, blue sucker, rotgut minnow, doughbelly

Scientific name:
Campostoma, Greek for "curved mouth"
anomalum, Latin for "extraordinary"

Distribution: Widespread in the eastern United States; common in streams of the southern High Plains. Absent from North Dakota and the Atlantic and Gulf coasts.

Size: Usually 3–6 inches to a maximum of about 8 inches.

Status: The central stoneroller is not threatened in any state.

The central stoneroller can be recognized by its distinctive profile, which consists of a rather long and bulbous snout and a horrendous overbite. The homely appearance of the stoneroller has not prevented it from becoming one of the more widespread and abundant minnows in the Midwest. Two other species of stonerollers occur in North America, and one of these, the largescale stoneroller, is also found in the central United States.

Stonerollers are characteristic of permanent streams with rocky riffles. Central stonerollers are common in small streams, whereas largescale stonerollers are more abundant in the larger streams of the Ozarks. Both species eat algae and any other encrusted organisms they can scrape from submerged objects with their hard, cartilaginous lower lip. In the Great Plains, stonerollers reach their greatest abundance in rocky, organically enriched streams that have thick growths of attached algae on rocks or gravel.

Male stonerollers fashion spawning pits in gravelly riffles, removing some gravel by mouth and "bulldozing" or "rolling" the larger stones with its head. The pits are usually near pools, where females wait and rest in relative safety. The eggs are adhesive and attach to stones in the nest. The parents abandon the eggs before they hatch.

The stoneroller shares the nickname of rotgut minnow with the common shiner, for both species spoil quickly when they are removed from water. Stonerollers are an important forage fish and also are occasionally used for bait. We have found them to be rather listless and shortlived on the hook, with no utility as bait for catfishes.

Suckers

Family CATOSTOMIDAE

*I never skin a sucker without admiring the
prismatic beauty of his scales.*
—*O. Henry*
  A Tempered Wind

The sucker family is probably one of the least understood and most persecuted groups of fishes in North America. The name *sucker* undoubtedly originated with the family's "vacuum cleaner–like" feeding habits, but it has since derived a special connotation for those of us with little or no common sense! There are approximately 65 species of suckers worldwide, principally limited to the waters of North America. The suckers may have evolved in eastern Asia and through geological time expanded their range across the Bering Sea to North America. Asian suckers are known only as fossils, except for one species in China and our own longnose sucker, which occurs also in Siberia.

Most suckers are bottom dwellers, using their ventral mouths to glean invertebrates and algae from lake and river bottoms. Adult suckers are typically "big" fishes, and most species in the central United States grow to lengths of a foot or more.

Coldwater suckers have received bad reputations via the disinformation network, which says suckers eat trout eggs and consume invertebrates that might otherwise be eaten by trout. Longnose suckers and mountain suckers do compete to a modest degree with trouts for food, living space, and spawning sites, but suckers and trout coexisted for eons before people decided they should not. Suckers are an integral component of the food web; they help to convert micro-organisms into flesh and are themselves valuable forage for adult trout.

Suckers are taken as food or sport fish in some regions of the country. Long ago, suckers were harvested in great numbers during their spring spawning runs and salted for later use. This practice prompted the well-known quote from Hardin Taliaferro: "I'm thirsty as a sucker in a salt bale." The utility of small suckers as food is limited by their many small bones, but the flesh can be scored crosswise with a sharp knife to facilitate softening of bones during cooking.

Blue Sucker

Cycleptus elongatus

Plate 69

Colloquial names: Missouri sucker, gourdseed sucker, suckerel, slenderhead sucker, bluefish, sweet sucker, blackhorse, schooner, long buffalo

Scientific name:
Cycleptus, "small round mouth" according to Rafinesque, perhaps Greek *cyclus* for "circle" and *leptes* for "a receiver" *elongatus,* Latin for "slender"

Distribution: In drainages from the Rio Grande to Mobile Bay, Alabama, including most large rivers of the Mississippi River system.

Size: Commonly growing to 3 pounds, to a maximum of 3 feet and 10 pounds. Formerly reached 20 pounds. The world record for hook-and-line is 14 lbs. 3 oz., taken from the Mississippi river in Minnesota in 1987.

Status: Protected or of special concern in most states along the periphery of its range, including the Dakotas, Minnesota, Wisconsin, Kansas, New Mexico, and Texas in the central United States.

The sleek blue sucker is well adapted for life in strong currents of big rivers and is most abundant within riffles or the narrowed constrictions of rapidly flowing chutes. The slender, flattened body of the blue sucker is wonderfully designed for minimal resistance to flow and enables it to hold steady in currents that would sweep most other fishes downstream. Although the blue sucker can tolerate turbid water, the species requires gravel or rock bottoms that are maintained relatively silt free by strong and constant flow. Construction of locks and dams on some of our larger rivers has blocked the spawning migrations of the blue sucker and inundated its habitat, allowing silt to settle over the bottom where the current has been slowed. Although blue suckers will sometimes congregate and feed in the swift water below dams, the overall impact of river modifications has been a decline in the number of blue suckers.

Blue suckers feed on algae and invertebrates that live on the river bottom. The species migrates upstream to spawn and scatters its eggs over a gravelly bottom in the current of riffles. As in other suckers, no care is given to the young. Breeding males are a striking blue-black and have their heads and bodies covered with small white tubercles.

The blue sucker has the reputation of being the tastiest of all the suckers and is consequently known as sweet sucker. The species was an important food fish before river modifications reduced its populations, and specimens weighing 20 pounds or more were not uncommon in the Mississippi and Missouri rivers.

Bigmouth Buffalo

Ictiobus cyprinellus

Plate 63

Colloquial names: common buffalo, gourdhead buffalo, redmouth buffalofish, stubnose buffalo, mud buffalo, lake buffalo, slough buffalo

Scientific name:
Ictiobus, Greek for "bull fish"
cyprinellus, Latin for "small carp"

Distribution: Throughout much of the Mississippi River drainage and its larger tributaries. Largely absent from the High Plains, except along the Missouri, Arkansas, and Red rivers.

Size: Commonly growing to 30 inches and 15 pounds, but 30–40 pound fish are not unusual. The world record weighed 70 lbs. 5 oz. and was caught in Bussey Brake, Louisiana, in April 1980.

Status: Not threatened in any state.

The bigmouth buffalo is the largest and most important commercial species among the suckers. Occasionally reaching a weight of 50 pounds, the bigmouth buffalo grows rapidly in the southern states and has a high production potential in commercial ponds even without supplemental feeding. The bigmouth is generally regarded as less palatable than the black or smallmouth buffaloes and is usually the least expensive in the marketplace. But the bigmouth's availability, low price, and good flavor when smoked make it one of the more popular market fishes in the central United States.

Bigmouth buffalo prosper in the warm, sluggish waters of large rivers and bayous and are exceedingly abundant in many shallow lakes, sloughs, oxbows, and other floodplain waters. The adult bigmouth has an obliquely slanted mouth or "bulldog's profile" and is thus less suited to bottom-feeding than the smallmouth and black buffaloes. The bigmouth buffalo takes more of its food from the "middle water" of lakes and streams where it filters tiny, free floating zooplankton from the water. The bigmouth occasionally plucks insect larvae or algae from the river bottom and is only rarely taken on hook-and-line, some catches being merely a result of accidental ingestion or snagging. Some anglers fish for bigmouth buffaloes by molding dough-baits around their hooks, a bait that hides the sharp hooks from the buffalo's sensitive lips.

Buffalofishes usually spawn in the spring after heavy rains, when they crowd into tributary streams and flooded marshes in extraordinary migrations. Typically, three or more males will congregate around a spawning female. When the female sinks to the bottom to release her eggs, the males crowd under and around her, pushing her to the surface of the water. The fish then "boil" the water in a spectacular, raucous rush, before sinking to the bottom and repeating the performance.

Black Buffalo

Ictiobus niger

Plate 64

Colloquial names: current buffalo, mongrel buffalo, prairie buffalo, chopper, blue rooter, round buffalo, bugler, chucklehead buffalo, buglemouth buffalo, buoy tender, deepwater buffalo

Scientific name:
Ictiobus, Greek for "bull fish"
niger, Latin for "dark" or "black"

Distribution: Mostly a fish of the Midwest in the Mississippi River and its larger tributaries. Largely absent from Minnesota, the Dakotas, and the High Plains from Nebraska through Texas.

Size: Commonly reaching 15 pounds, to a maximum of 50 pounds. The world record on hook-and-line weighed 52 pounds and was caught in the Mississippi River in Wisconsin in 1985.

Status: Protected or of special concern in some states, including South Dakota.

The black buffalo is intermediate in most respects to the bigmouth and smallmouth buffaloes and has sometimes been considered a hybrid between the two. It is usually not as abundant as the other two species.

The black buffalo was originally described in 1820 by Constantine Rafinesque, who had never seen the species and relied wholly upon the drawing and word of John James Audubon. But Rafinesque was fooled by Audubon's apocryphal Buffalo Carp Sucker (among a dozen or so other fake fishes) and also included that "species" in the same monograph.

The black buffalo is typically the darkest of the buffalofishes. Color is not, however, a diagnostic characteristic and cannot be accurately used to distinguish species of *Ictiobus.* For instance, a buffalo from the black, tea-stained waters of a swamp will be a dark blackish-bronze, in contrast to the same species from a shallow, sandy river where it assumes a protective coloration of light, brassy-brown. Like the other species of *Ictiobus,* the black buffalo draws its common name from its humpbacked nape. In contrast to the smallmouth buffalo, the back of the black buffalo is not keeled or as steeply arched, but positive identification of specimens less than 1 pound is difficult. Although the black and smallmouth buffaloes have similar habits and requirements, the black buffalo is more often found in deeper and stronger currents, hence its common names of buoy tender and current buffalo.

Smallmouth Buffalo

Ictiobus bubalus

Plate 65

Colloquial names: blue pancake, brown buffalo, suckermouth buffalo, rooter, razorback, quillback buffalo, white carp, round buffalo, humpbacked buffalo, liner, roachback

Scientific name:
Ictiobus, Greek for "bull fish"
bubalus, Greek for "buffalo"

Distribution: Throughout most of the Mississippi drainage, spreading west into the High Plains along the Arkansas and Red rivers and other large tributaries and occurring in the Dakotas and Montana in the Missouri River.

Size: On average, the smallest of the buffalofish, but commonly growing to 15 pounds; maximum weight about 40 pounds. The world record, caught from the Louisiana side of Toledo Bend Reservoir in 1989, weighed 79 lbs. 8 oz.

Status: Not threatened in any state.

Although not quite as abundant as the bigmouth buffalo, the smallmouth is a widespread and valuable commercial fish that brings a premium price in the market. The smallmouth buffalo's deep, "pancake" body, keeled back, and ventral or bottom-feeding mouth distinguish it from its big-mouthed relative. Young smallmouth buffalo (those less than 12 inches in total length) are difficult to distinguish from the black buffalo and are sometimes confused with the river carpsucker. In contrast to the carpsuckers, smallmouth buffaloes have a bronze tint and a rounded subopercle bone on the gill cover; the carpsuckers have a triangular subopercle.

The smallmouth buffalo typically inhabits clearer and faster-flowing waters than the bigmouth buffalo. An opportunistic feeder, the smallmouth will eat almost any bottom-dwelling organism that is abundant and easy to swallow. Insect larvae, attached algae, fingernail clams, crustaceans, and zooplankton are favorites. At night, schools of smallmouth buffalo sometimes feed with their backs exposed in shallow riffles, often in the company of black buffaloes. In aquaria, a smallmouth buffalo will suck sand and fine gravel into its mouth, clean the gravel of organisms, and then forcefully eject the substrate from its mouth. In contrast, the bigmouth buffalo strains silt and sand through its throat and out through the gill openings.

All three of our species of buffaloes are infrequently caught on hook-and-line but can be caught on river or lake bottoms by imbedding small hooks in doughballs, cottonseed cakes, or cheese. The initial strike and rush of the buffalo is strong, but it quickly drops the bait if its tender lips feel the hook or the resistance of the line.

River Carpsucker

Carpiodes carpio

Plate 66

Colloquial names: white carp, common river carp, silver carp

Scientific name:
Carpiodes, Latin for "carp-like"
carpio, Latin for "carp"

Distribution: Throughout rivers and reservoirs of the Great Plains, from northern Mexico to Montana and Minnesota.

Size: Growing to 24 inches and about 10 pounds. The hook-and-line record is 5 lbs. 12 oz., from Lake St. Clair in Michigan, caught in 1986.

Status: Not threatened in the central United States.

The river carpsucker is the most abundant and widespread of our carpsuckers, occurring mainly in quiet, silt-bottomed pools and slow, sandy runs of rivers. The species is also common in reservoirs, and large carpsuckers will emigrate upstream into tributary streams during high flow, much in the fashion of catfishes. The river carpsucker feeds on tiny aquatic worms, small crustaceans, and diatoms and other algae that it gleans from lake or stream bottoms. Despite its predilection for bottom "slime," the carpsucker is occasionally caught by anglers, who call it white carp, a disparaging nickname that has probably caused embarrassment to the entire sucker clan.

Carpsuckers hemorrhage easily when they are caught in a seine or net, a habit that causes their fins and sides to take on a reddish tinge. Carpsuckers are thick bodied and muscular and will thrash furiously in the bottom of boats. But once returned to the water, the temperamental carpsucker will usually go "fins up" and die.

Quillback

Carpiodes cyprinus
Plate 67

Colloquial names: carpsucker, American carp, silver carp, eastern carpsucker, plains carpsucker

Scientific name:
Carpiodes, Latin for "carp-like"
cyprinus, Greek name for "carp"

Distribution: North-central and northeastern United States and scattered from southern Manitoba to western Alberta. Most common in our range in Iowa, Nebraska, Missouri, and northern Arkansas.

Size: Up to 2 feet and 10 pounds.

Status: Not protected in any state.

The quillback is one of the most variable of all our fishes, but it can usually be separated from other carpsuckers by its slightly longer snout and the blunt apex of its lower lip. The quillback is similar to the river carpsucker but typically has a larger eye and lacks the river carpsucker's median knob or "pea-shaped swelling" in the center of its lower lip. Most eastern forms of the quillback (pictured) also have the first few rays of the dorsal fin long and falcate and extending almost to the back base of the dorsal fin. But the western subspecies (sometimes called plains carpsucker) has the first rays of the dorsal fin shortened as in the river carpsucker.

The quillback prefers clearer water than the river carpsucker and is usually more abundant in large rivers with gravel or other firm-bottomed substrates. Quillbacks feed on algae, small bloodworms, microscopic crustaceans, and other bottom "ooze" that accumulates in the slack waters of rivers. This species and other carpsuckers are occasionally eaten smoked, but they are full of small bones, hence the name "chokefishes."

Highfin Carpsucker

Carpiodes velifer

Plate 68

Colloquial names: skimback, sailing sucker, humpbacked carp, spearfish, sailor, bluntnose river carp

Scientific name:
Carpiodes, Latin for "carp-like"
velifer, Latin for "sail-bearer"

Distribution: South-central United States from southern Minnesota and Ohio to eastern Oklahoma, Alabama, and the Florida panhandle.

Size: Smallest of our carpsuckers, averaging about 12 inches and 1 pound, to a maximum of about 4 pounds.

Status: Protected in Kansas and Tennessee but declining throughout most of its range.

The highfin carpsucker is restricted to clear, sandy- or rocky-bottomed streams of the south-central United States. The highfin is distinguished from other *Carpiodes* by its deeper body and by a long, falcate dorsal fin having front rays that extend past the back end of the fin. Like other carpsuckers, the highfin avoids strong currents and feeds along the bottom of pools and embayments on diatoms and other algae. Highfins spawn in shallows or overflow waters of rivers and streams in late spring by broadcasting eggs over clean gravel substrate.

The highfin carpsucker has the peculiar practice of jumping clear of the water and skimming along the water's surface with its upper back and dorsal fin exposed. Thus, its common nicknames of skimback, sailing sucker, and—as Rafinesque proposed—"flying fish." The highfin carpsucker was a common fish in the early part of this century, but the species is now rare or threatened over much of its range. The decline of the highfin carpsucker is presumed to be a result of increased turbidity and siltation.

Longnose Sucker

Catostomus catostomus

Plate 70

Colloquial names: sturgeon sucker, northern sucker, redside sucker

Scientific name:
Catostomus, Greek for "mouth below"

Distribution: Canada south into the United States in Rocky Mountains, Great Lakes region, and New England. Also in eastern Siberia. In our region, restricted to the upper Missouri in North Dakota and Montana, Spearfish Creek in the Black Hills, much of Wyoming and Colorado, and several streams in western Nebraska.

Size: Up to about 25 inches, but average about 16 inches. The world record for hook-and-line is 6 lbs. 14 oz., caught in the St. Joseph River of Michigan in 1986.

Status: Protected in South Dakota and of special concern in other states, including North Dakota.

The long, slender body and Roman profile are distinctive trademarks of the longnose sucker, a species that is the only sucker native to North America and Asia. The longnose prefers cold, clear water but is tolerant of the warmer, more turbid waters of lakes and streams in the northern High Plains.

Longnose suckers spawn in late spring or summer, oftentimes near spawning trout, and are thought to eat unburied trout eggs from overcrowded nesting sites. The longnose, however, feeds principally on algae, and consequently the young suckers are valuable as forage for trout.

The male longnose sucker is a handsome fish; he develops a bright red lateral stripe during the breeding season in late spring or early summer. The species is occasionally used as bait and has extended its range through bait-bucket releases. The longnose sucker is long lived (20 years) and a fair food fish, sometimes being used as food for domestic animals—although Scott and Crossman, in *Freshwater Fishes of Canada*, suggest that even dogs prefer lake whitefish.

Mountain Sucker

Catostomus platyrhynchus

Plate 71

Colloquial names: redside sucker, Jordan's sucker

Scientific name:
Catostomus, Greek for "mouth below"
platyrhynchus, Greek for "flat snout"

Distribution: Mountainous regions of western North America from California and Colorado to British Columbia and Saskatchewan. Coming into our region in Wyoming, eastern Montana, the Black Hills, and a few Pine Ridge streams in northwest Nebraska.

Size: Usually 6–8 inches, to a maximum of 12 inches.

Status: Uncommon in Nebraska, but not threatened within the central United States.

As its name suggests, the mountain sucker is at home in cold, clear streams (and a few lakes) of the mountains, although it is also found sparingly within cold-water streams of the northern Great Plains in Nebraska, Wyoming, Montana, and the Black Hills of South Dakota. The species is most at home in small streams with aquatic vegetation or deeply undercut banks. Mountain suckers have bumpy (papillose) lips as do the longnose and white suckers, but the lower and upper lips of the mountain sucker are separated by a notch. Cartilaginous edges on the lower jaw makes this species well adapted to scraping algae from rocks, and animal matter composes only a tiny percentage of its diet. James Simon (in Baxter and Simon's *Wyoming Fishes*) reported that these suckers have the odd habit of turning themselves upside down to feed on the algal growth attached to the underside of large boulders.

Not much is known about the spawning behavior of mountain suckers. Like the longnose suckers, breeding males develop orange or bright red stripes along their midsides. Mountain suckers are small fishes, mostly less than 1 pound, but are sometimes used as bait or as food for captive furbearing animals.

White Sucker

Catostomus commersoni

Plate 72

Colloquial names: common sucker, brook sucker, mud sucker, black sucker, gray sucker, mullet, black mullet, June sucker

Scientific name:
Catostomus, Greek for "mouth below" *commersoni,* named for French naturalist Philibert Commerson

Distribution: Much of northeastern North America from the Northwest Territories to the Atlantic Coast, south through North Carolina to New Mexico, becoming less common in the southern High Plains.

Size: About 10–16 inches. The world record for hook-and-line weighed 7 lbs. 4 oz. and was caught in 1978 from Big Round Lake in Wisconsin.

Status: Not threatened in any state.

Within the central United States, the white sucker can be found in most types of streams and lakes, but it seems to prefer different habitats in the various parts of its range. In Kansas and Missouri, white suckers are encountered most often in small streams with well-defined pools and riffles. In Minnesota and Wisconsin it is widely distributed in both streams and lakes. Adult suckers are omnivorous, feeding on plants, algae, crustaceans, and larval insects.

In spring, white suckers make upstream spawning runs, congregating near riffles. Two males will usually move alongside a ripe female, and as the eggs are deposited, the trio vibrates, stirring up the gravel and sand and burying the eggs. White suckers are relatively long-lived fish, with life spans of 15 years or more.

The white sucker is occasionally caught on hook-and-line and has economic value as a food fish for people and animals. White suckers are also used as bait, and a fat, 12-inch specimen is the most popular bait for muskie and pike in our northern and Great Lakes states.

Black Redhorse

Moxostoma duquesnei

Plate 73

Colloquial names: Pittsburgh sucker, bigjawed sucker

Scientific name:
Moxostoma, Greek for "sucking mouth"
duquesnei, Latinized for Fort Duquesne, near Pittsburgh

Distribution: Black redhorses occur in the Ozarks, the Ohio River system, the upper Mobile Bay drainage, the upper Mississippi River basin, and the southern Great Lakes drainages.

Size: Adults usually 7–15 inches.

Status: Protected or of special concern in some states, including Iowa, Kansas, and Minnesota.

Black redhorses typically inhabit the gravelly or rocky runs and pools of clear and cool perennial streams. The species has a very low tolerance of turbidity and has disappeared or become uncommon in many silted streams. This species lacks red or orange pigment in the dorsal and caudal fins, as does the golden redhorse. The black redhorse's pronounced upper lip, curved profile, and slender caudal peduncle distinguish it from the golden redhorse. The black redhorse is relatively long lived and might reach 10 years of age and 2 pounds in weight. The diet of this redhorse consists of a variety of small mollusks, immature insects, crustaceans, and algae.

Like other redhorses, the black redhorse spawns in April or May in shallow riffles. Breeding males develop tubercles over their bodies and establish territories about their spawning shoals. Two males will usually spawn with one female. William Pflieger, in his *The Fishes of Missouri,* reports that prior to spawning, black redhorses will congregate in pools near riffles to participate in a jumping routine during which they continuously leap clear of the water. This peculiar ritual signals the start of the brief, week-long spawning period.

Golden Redhorse

Moxostoma erythrurum

Plate 74

Colloquial names: common redhorse, smallheaded mullet

Scientific name:
Moxostoma, Greek for "sucking mouth"
erythrurum, Greek for "red tailed," a misnomer

Distribution: Golden redhorses are generally distributed in the upper and middle Mississippi and Mobile Bay drainages to the southern Great Lakes. Largely absent from the Dakotas and Nebraska but common in eastern Kansas and Oklahoma. Isolated populations occur in southwestern Mississippi and in Virginia and North Carolina.

Size: Adults usually 7–15 inches, to a maximum of 26 inches.

Status: The golden redhorse is of special concern in South Dakota and Manitoba.

The golden redhorse is named appropriately for its array of gilded scales. Unfortunately, most of the other *Moxostoma* species are similarly attired and are not readily distinguishable from the golden redhorse on the basis of scale color. The golden redhorse can be distinguished from the shorthead and river redhorses by its tail and dorsal fins, which *lack* red pigments, contrary to its specific epithet *erythrurum*, which means "red-tailed"! During the spring breeding season, the male golden redhorse grows pointed tubercles on the head and develops a larger, more rounded anal fin.

Golden redhorses are typically found in stream pools that have firm bottoms of sand or silt and are commonly found cohabiting streams with the black redhorse. However, the golden redhorse is more tolerant of warm temperatures and moderate turbidity, and it thus occurs farther west onto the Great Plains.

The golden redhorse feeds on larval insects, algae, and other organisms associated with hard substrates. Anglers occasionally catch golden redhorses on hook-and-line using worms or small jigs, but the species' slow, deliberate manner usually precludes more than one passive tug on the line.

Shorthead Redhorse

Moxostoma macrolepidotum

Plate 75

Colloquial names: northern redhorse, redfin sucker, red mullet, eastern redhorse, river sucker, brook mullet, common mullet, Des Moines plunger

Scientific name:
Moxostoma, Greek for "sucking mouth"
macrolepidotum, Greek for "large scaled"

Distribution: The shorthead redhorse is the most widely distributed species of redhorse, found from Alberta to the St. Lawrence River and south from Oklahoma to South Carolina.

Size: Adults usually 8–16 inches, to a maximum of about 24 inches. The world record weighed 11 lbs. 5 oz. and was caught on the Brunet River in Wisconsin.

Status: Not protected in the central United States.

The shorthead redhorse resembles the river redhorse but has a relatively small head, and the posterior edge of its bottom lip is straight or convex. Shortheads are found in moderate-sized streams, natural lakes, and reservoirs. In streams, they have a decided preference for perennial flows but are tolerant of turbidity and can withstand short periods of intermittent flows.

The large size of the shorthead redhorse makes the species one of our most popular "sport suckers." Worms are a popular "on purpose" bait for the shorthead in our more northern states and are generally fished on the bottom in pools or eddies.

As do most species of redhorses, shortheads migrate upstream to gravelly riffles in the spring to spawn. This species, along with the golden redhorse, is probably responsible for the denomination of Illinois as the Sucker State, for the first settlers emigrated into the area in the spring during the annual spawning runs of the suckers.

River Redhorse

Moxostoma carinatum

Plate 76

Colloquial names: bigtoothed redhorse, bigjawed redhorse

Scientific name:
Moxostoma, Greek for "sucking mouth"
carinatum, Latin for "keel"

Distribution: Principally west of the Appalachians in the Ohio and Tennessee river valleys, the Missouri, Oklahoma, and Arkansas Ozarks, and the northern Mississippi Valley.

Size: Adults usually 1–2 feet, to a maximum of about 8 pounds.

Status: Protected or of special concern over much of its range, including Iowa and Kansas.

The river redhorse is a large sucker with a chubby head and stocky body. It is most similar in appearance to the shorthead redhorse but has a relatively larger head and a V-shaped indentation on the posterior edge of the lower lip. River redhorses often have a thin, vertical black line at the base of their bright-red tails, a character that sometimes fades with age. The river redhorse frequents clean, permanent streams and is usually found in pools having gravel or bedrock bottoms. The species also occurs in a few reservoirs and natural lakes.

Although most redhorses have slender, comblike teeth on their gill arches to aid with feeding, the river redhorse has large, molarlike throat teeth that are designed to crush clams, mussels, and snails. Because both the river redhorse and the clams on which it feeds are sensitive to turbidity and pollution, the river redhorse has disappeared from much of its former range and is now one of our most uncommon suckers.

Spawning behavior of the river redhorse is similar to that of the white sucker and the other redhorses. River redhorses fashion nests in the gravel, using their tails, mouths, and heads to rearrange small stones. River redhorses often live for 10 years or more.

Gray Redhorse

Moxostoma congestum

Plate 77

Colloquial names: Texas redhorse

Scientific name:
Moxostoma, Greek for "sucking mouth"
congestum, Latin for "swollen," probably a
reference to the "full" lower lip

Distribution: The gray redhorse is one of
the few southwestern species of redhorse
and lives in southern Texas, southeastern
New Mexico, and northeastern Mexico.

Size: Adults usually 9–13 inches, to a maximum of about 20 inches.

Status: Endangered in New Mexico.

The gray redhorse is a native of the southwestern United States where it inhabits
rocky-, sandy-, or gravel-bottomed pools
and deep runs of creeks and rivers. The
species has also been found in a few lakes
in Texas. The young and subadults of the
gray redhorse are loosely gregarious and inhabit riffles and gravelly runs. The gray
redhorse prefers relatively clear, warm
water and is most abundant in the Edwards
Plateau region of south-central Texas,
where it occurs in the company of the native guadalupe bass. The gray redhorse is
the only species of *Moxostoma* in New Mexico and is the common redhorse of southwestern Texas. The black-banded membranes in the dorsal and caudal fins of the
gray redhorse distinguish it from all of our
other species of redhorses.

Gray redhorses subsist on larval insects,
crayfish, snails, and small clams. The gray
redhorse is thought to spawn in riffles, and
the spawning regimen is probably similar to
that of the other redhorses. Like other
moxostomids, breeding males develop fine
tubercles about the head and an enlarged,
tuberculate anal fin in the spring.

Northern Hog Sucker

Hypentelium nigricans
Plate 78

Colloquial names: hogmolly, hognose sucker, hog mullet, black sucker, stone-roller, stonetoter, stonelugger, hammer-head, boxhead, riffle sucker

Scientific name:
Hypentelium, Greek for "below 5 lobes," a reference to the lower lip
nigricans, Latin for "blackish"

Distribution: Mississippi and Ohio river drainages, the Great Lakes drainage, and Atlantic Coast drainages from New York to northern Georgia. Most common in our region in the Missouri and Arkansas Ozarks.

Size: From 5–15 inches and about 2 pounds.

Status: Of special concern in Kansas and South Dakota.

The large bony head, fleshy lips, and long, slender body of the comical hog sucker give it all the appearance of Mother Nature's version of the handheld vacuum. For some unknown reason, the northern hog sucker received the tag of "mud sucker" in the nineteenth century. The species is now known to inhabit almost exclusively the riffles or pools of clear, permanent streams with bottoms of gravel or rock. The hog sucker's reduced swim bladder, ventral mouth, and large pectoral fins mark it strictly as a bottom dweller. Adult hog suckers are not as strongly inclined to school as are other suckers but are occasionally found in loose-knit aggregations of four or five fish. Hog suckers are active feeders, frequently moving stones with their large heads and sucking up the exposed materials, spitting out the undigestable and swallowing any aquatic insects. The species' foraging behavior is so disruptive to the bottom fauna that turtles and other species of fish have developed a behavior pattern of following the hog sucker and feasting on the leftovers.

Spawning behavior of the hog sucker is similar to that described for the white sucker. One or more males will shimmy against the female in a gravelly riffle, stirring the substrate and helping to fertilize and mix the eggs among the gravel. Hog suckers are normally skittish fishes that dart away when approached, their mottled coloration blending well with the rocky substrate and rendering them invisible. However, during the spawning period, hog suckers lose their characteristic shyness and, according to William Pflieger in his *The Fishes of Missouri,* can sometimes be captured or "noodled" from the water by hand.

Spotted Sucker

Minytrema melanops

Plate 79

Colloquial names: striped sucker, speckled sucker, sand sucker, winter sucker, black sucker, spotted redhorse, corncob sucker

Scientific name:
Minytrema, Greek for "reduced aperture," a reference to the reduced lateral line
melanops, Greek for "black appearance"

Distribution: Gulf and Atlantic coast drainages from Texas to North Carolina, including much of the Mississippi River valley, and lower Great Lakes drainages. In our range mostly in southern Missouri, southeast Kansas, Arkansas, and eastern Oklahoma.

Size: Adults from 6 to 19 inches.

Status: Reduced in number in parts of its range but considered of special concern only in Kansas and Ontario.

The spotted sucker is the only species of the genus *Minytrema* and is our only sucker with a "checkerboard" pattern on its back and sides. Spotted suckers typically live in sluggish, low-gradient streams with soft bottoms of silt, organic debris, or sand. They are often found near vegetation and have a pronounced predilection for water that is clear or only slightly dingy. In recent years, spotted suckers have become uncommon over much of their former range, probably a result of increased stream turbidity. Nineteenth-century ichthyologist Edward Drinker Cope once recommended the striped sucker for domestication because of its hardiness in the aquarium.

During the spring spawn, male spotted suckers develop tuberculate heads and establish territories in riffles. One or more males will accompany the female in the spawning ritual, and fertilized eggs drift downstream and sink to the bottom, eventually being concealed by the sand and debris that are stirred up by the spawning fish.

The spotted sucker has little economic value but is occasionally angled by "worm" anglers, who consider its flesh to be delicious. During the spawning runs of the nineteenth century, spotted suckers and redhorses were often captured from clear waters with simple snares of horsehair or fine wire.

Creek Chubsucker and Lake Chubsucker

Erimyzon oblongus and *Erimyzon sucetta*

Plates 80–81

Colloquial names: Creek chubsucker—chub sucker, creekfish, creek sucker, barbel Lake chubsucker—chub sucker, sweet sucker, pin sucker, pin minnow

Scientific name:
Erimyzon, Greek for "to suck"
oblongus, Latin for "oblong" (creek chubsucker)
sucetta, French for "sucker" (lake chubsucker)

Distribution: Both species in Mississippi Valley and other nearby Gulf Coast drainages north to Great Lakes region. Creek chubsucker also found in Atlantic Coast drainages from Georgia through New England. Lake chubsucker more southerly along Atlantic Coast, from Florida to southern Virginia. Both species coming into our range in southern Missouri, Arkansas, and east Texas.

Size: Creek chubsucker usually 4.5–7 inches. Lake chubsucker normally 5–11 inches.

Status: The lake chubsucker is protected or of special concern in several states, including Iowa and Missouri. The creek chubsucker is protected only in Texas.

The chubsuckers are little-known and rather obscure suckers that prefer clear, vegetated waters with little or no flow and a sand or silt bottom overlain by organic debris. The lake chubsucker is found in river pools, oxbows, and impoundments, whereas the creek chubsucker is generally restricted to the pools of small creeks, ponded overflow waters, or river backwaters. The chubsuckers are sensitive to muddy waters and have disappeared from some parts of their ranges as a result of the increased loads of silt in the streams. Neither species is very abundant at any site in the central United States.

Chubsuckers feed on invertebrates, but unlike most other suckers, they have subterminal mouths, which suggests that they are not restricted to bottom feeding. The spawning behavior of the creek chubsucker is similar to that of the white sucker. The species moves upstream into riffles, and the female scatters her eggs over the gravel substrate. There is some evidence that males form a pseudo-nest or spawning depression by rearranging stones in the spawning area. Spawning in the lake chubsucker is similar to that of the creek chubsucker, but in some lakes or ponds the lake chubsucker might scatter its eggs over submerged vegetation.

In much of the central United States, the chubsuckers are too uncommon to be of much value. Elsewhere, they are important forage fish and bait fish and are occasionally taken on hook-and-line. The young of both species strongly resemble minnows and have a dark lateral pinstripe on each side, hence the common name pin minnow. Creek chubsuckers are legally protected in Texas, and the lake chubsucker is of special concern in most of its western periphery.

Catfishes

Family ICTALURIDAE

Do not tell fish stories where the people know you; but particularly, don't tell them where they know the fish.
—Mark Twain

The catfish is famous for its smooth scaleless skin, adipose fin, and unshaven "whiskered" face. Nowhere is it unrecognized, and its abundance, ease of capture, and simple palatal pleasures embody the entire idealism of fishing. The family comprises 37 species, which encompass a wide range of sizes. Two species, the blue and flathead catfishes, exceed 100 pounds, yet most of the bullheads will typically grow no longer than 15 inches. The madtoms are smaller still, with most species growing to a maximum of 5 inches or less. Prior to transplantings, the entire distribution of the ictalurid catfishes was restricted to North America. Although catfishes have been widely introduced into western states, none of our species are native west of the Rocky Mountains.

The catfish takes its name from the four pairs of long, flexible barbels or "cat whiskers" on its head. Replete with taste buds (which are found on the skin and fins as well), the barbels help the catfish to test the taste and feel of objects and enable it to locate food in turbid water. Contrary to myth, the whiskers of the catfish are harmless to the touch. However, catfishes can inflict painful wounds with their sharply pointed pectoral and dorsal spines, and some species have small venom glands at the bases of these fins. Curiously, the venom of the madtoms, the smallest of the catfishes, produces the most painful wound. When alarmed, a catfish will rigidly lock its spines at right angles to its body, a formidable posture that repels most predators or intruders.

Catfishes spawn in natural cavities or depressions along river banks, in or around brush or rocks, or perhaps even in discarded automobile tires or beer cans. The male assumes the role of guardian and watches over the eggs and young until the latter are several weeks old.

Our larger catfishes, especially the bullheads, seem tolerant of any improprieties ranging from siltation and pollution to low oxygen and cold morning coffee. The bullheads' predilection for dingy waters helps to maintain a fishery in many of the small, muddy creeks of the Great Plains. "Any water," said David Starr Jordan, "which does not dry up absolutely to the bottom in summer will suffice to nurture the common small catfishes."

Black Bullhead

Ictalurus melas

Plate 82

Colloquial names: bullhead, mudcat, slick, common bullhead, horned pout, yellowbelly bullhead, polliwog, stinger, chucklehead, river snapper

Scientific name:
Ictalurus, Greek for "fish cat"
melas, Greek for "black"

Distribution: Throughout the central United States, absent from the East Coast, introduced along the Pacific Coast. Our most common bullhead.

Size: Usually 1 pound or less, but occasionally growing to 2 pounds in ponds or swamps. The world record of 8 lbs. 15 oz. was caught in Sturgis Pond, Michigan, in August 1987.

Status: Not protected in any state.

The black bullhead is decidedly a youngster's fish, seemingly more at home on the hook than in its free and natural state. Being a scavenger, the bullhead will pounce upon any offering of edibles with an abandoned exuberance, and because it forbears from any pretense of caution, it has championed all other fishes at "swallowing the hook"! The name *bullhead* was supposedly derived from the name as applied to freshwater sculpins in England, for both groups have similarly oversized heads. We think the name equally appropriate for the bullheaded stubbornness with which this catfish accedes to its own capture.

The black bullhead spawns in late spring or early summer, and one parent will usually watch over the fry until the young are about 1 inch long. Scores of young bullheads can be seen in early summer schooled into a compact mass, swimming and changing direction as though of one mind.

The fewer anal fin rays (17–21) and the smooth or only slightly serrated pectoral spines distinguish the black bullhead from its look-alike cousins. The black bullhead is a hardy fish and is abundant in sluggish streams and muddy stagnant ponds, where it is tolerant of warm water and low oxygen. Accordingly, the black bullhead is usually the last species of fish in a High Plains stream to succumb to drought. Many of the shallow, muddy streams occupied by the black bullhead are unproductive in terms of natural foods (insects and crustaceans), and the bullheads are characteristically overpopulated and stunted in growth.

Yellow Bullhead

Ictalurus natalis

Plate 83

Colloquial names: yellow cat, yellowbelly bullhead, brown bullhead, butterball, buttercat, polliwog, greaser, Mississippi bullhead, paper skin, white-whiskered bullhead, slick bullhead

Scientific name:

Ictalurus, Greek for "fish cat"

natalis, Latin for "having large buttocks," so named by Lesueur for his obese specimens

Distribution: Native and common in the eastern half of the United States, becoming uncommon in the High Plains from western North Dakota to west Texas.

Size: Commonly 6–12 inches long, occasionally reaching a weight of 2 pounds. The world record on hook-and-line weighed 4 lbs. 8 oz. and was caught in Mormon Lake, Arizona, in 1989.

Status: Of special concern in North Dakota.

"The horned pout," wrote Henry David Thoreau of the bullheads,

> are dull and blundering fellows, fond of the mud and growing best in weedy ponds and rivers without much current. They stay near the bottom, moving slowly about with their barbels spread, watching for anything eatable. They will take any kind of bait, from an angleworm to a piece of tomato can, without hesitation or coquetry, and they seldom fail to swallow the hook. They are very tenacious of life, opening and shutting their mouth for half an hour after their heads have been taken off.

The yellow bullhead has much the same habits and range as the black bullhead. Similar in size and color to its black cousin, the yellow bullhead can be distinguished by its creamy white chin barbels (compared to gray or black of the black bullhead) and by its longer anal fin (24–27 rays). Astute students of ichthyology who have developed "fish eyes" from seeing many specimens also can recognize the shorter and relatively wider heads of the yellow bullhead.

Yellow bullheads have a predilection for clearer waters and a firm substrate of sand, gravel, or rock. Nevertheless, black and yellow bullheads sometimes cohabit the same muddy pool. The yellow bullhead is most abundant in the clear backwaters of Missouri Ozark streams, the shallow lakes of Iowa and Minnesota, and the sandy rivers of the central Plains.

Yellow bullheads are on average a bit larger than black bullheads, because of the latter species' tendency to overpopulate and stunt. The yellow bullhead is sometimes referred to as greaser or slick bullhead by anglers because its thick layer of mucus and paper-thin hide make it difficult to skin.

Brown Bullhead

Ictalurus nebulosus

Plate 84

Colloquial names: common bullhead, horned pout, common pout, bullpout, speckled bullhead, marbled bullhead, Schuylkill cat, wooly cat, red cat, Sacramento cat

Scientific name:
Ictalurus, Greek for "fish cat"
nebulosus, Latin for "clouded," a reference to the mottled sides

Distribution: Mostly ranging to the east of the Mississippi River, spreading westward into Minnesota, Arkansas, and Louisiana. Introduced into many rivers in California and Oregon.

Size: Averages slightly larger than the other bullheads, but generally less than 2 pounds. The world record, caught from Veal Pond in Georgia in 1975, weighed 5 lbs. 8 oz.

Status: Of special concern in Missouri.

The bullhead clan owes the origin of its dubious reputation to the brown bullhead, for it is the common horned pout of the eastern United States and the first fish of many young anglers in that region. The name *horned pout* stems from the bullhead's habit of locking its pectoral fins or "horns" at right angles to its body: *pout* having a Middle English derivative meaning "fish

with a large head." Wrote George W. Peck of the phenomenon in the *Milwaukee Sun* during the nineteenth century:

> There is one drawback to the bullhead, and that is his horns. We doubt if a boy ever descended into the patent insides of a bullhead to mine for limerick hooks, that did not, before his work was done, run a horn into his vital parts. But the boy seems to expect it and the bullhead enjoys it. We have seen a bullhead lie on the bank and become dry, and to all appearances dead to all that was going on, and when a boy sat down on him and got a horn in his elbow and yelled murder, the bullhead would grin from ear to ear, and wag his tail as though applauding for an encore.

The brown bullhead is absent from the Great Plains and much of the central United States, although it is common in lakes and streams through much of Minnesota, in the swampy backwaters of Louisiana and Arkansas, and in Mingo Swamp in southeastern Missouri. Its habits are similar to those of the black bullhead with which it occasionally hybridizes.

The brown bullhead's catholic tastes and propensity for swallowing "hook, line, and sinker" are unmatched outside of the other bullheads. When other fishes refuse to bite, the angler so disposed will always find the bullhead willing to cooperate.

Channel Catfish

Ictalurus punctatus
Plates 85–87

Colloquial names: fiddler, spotted cat, blue channel, blue cat, speckled cat, Great Lakes catfish, willow cat, blue fulton, chucklehead

Scientific name:
Ictalurus, Greek for "fish cat"
punctatus, Latin for "spotted," reference to the spots on young specimens

Distribution: Originally abundant throughout the Mississippi drainage, Great Lakes, and much of southeastern Canada. Now throughout the continental United States, Hawaii, and Great Britain.

Size: Commonly to 10 pounds. The world record channel catfish was 47.5 inches long and weighed 58 lbs, caught from Santee Cooper Reservoir of South Carolina in July 1964.

Status: Not threatened in any state.

Few other warm-water sport fishes have an allegiant following like the channel catfish. The most widespread and abundant of all our catfishes, the channel cat has probably produced more good will for the ictalurids than all other catfishes combined.

The channel catfish's exceeding variability in color and form has caused a great deal of confusion and misidentifications among fishermen as well as ichthyologists. Young channel catfish (often called fiddlers) are greenish in color with dark spots and have their anal and caudal fins outlined with black pigment. Mature females are often a coppery brown or silvery gray, but adult males sport a dark blue or gray cast and develop thickened lips and head muscles during the breeding season. On the basis of their sexual and geographic variability, male channel catfish were once thought to be several different species, the so-called Great Lakes, willow, and eel catfishes. Not until the 1940s were these "species" determined simply to be variations of plain old *Ictalurus punctatus*!

Anglers still confuse the channel cat with the blue catfish. Both blue catfish and breeding male channel cats are sometimes termed chuckleheads, and male channel cats are more often mistakenly called blue catfish! Although most juvenile channel catfish can be differentiated by their spotted sides, the spots are more or less obscured in large adults. A channel catfish can be distinguished by its shorter and more rounded anal fin, which has from 24 to 29 rays, as opposed to the 30 to 35 in the blue catfish.

The channel catfish is not finicky and will bite at almost any type of bait, occasionally even a plug or spinner. Its natural foods consist of insects, freshwater clams, snails, fish, algae, and even cottonwood seeds, but large adults eat mostly fish. We have caught channel catfish on june bugs, worms, crayfish, live fish, and even rotting jumbo shrimp from the Gulf Coast. The redolent "stink baits," be they homemade, commercially prepared, or of the Gulf Coast shrimp variety, are particularly effective because of the many "taste buds" on the skin and whiskers of the channel cat.

The channel catfish is more likely to be found in or around the edges of flowing water than either of our other large catfishes, the blue or flathead cats. Channels are most active under the cover of darkness, and many "cat" anglers run their setlines, trotlines, or juglines only at night. A sudden and steady rise in creeks and rivers triggers feeding and wanderlust in channel catfish, and members of the species will swim many miles upstream from reservoirs during times of high flow, creating an excellent, albeit temporary, fishing resource.

Blue Catfish

Ictalurus furcatus
Plate 88

Colloquial names: white fulton, blue fulton, great blue cat, chucklehead, Mississippi cat, fulton, humpback blue, white cat, blue channel cat, highfin blue, forktail cat

Scientific name:
Ictalurus, Greek for "fish cat"
furcatus, Latin for "forked," a reference to the tail

Distribution: Occurring in the Mississippi River and its larger tributaries; native to much of southern Texas and into southeast New Mexico via the Rio Grande and Pecos River.

Size: Reached 150 pounds or more in the nineteenth century. Today, few specimens reach 60 pounds, and most "large" blue cats weigh 30–40 pounds. The world record for hook-and-line weighed 97 lbs. and was caught in 1959 from the Missouri River in South Dakota.

Status: Of special concern in Minnesota and West Virginia and uncommon over much of its former range in the Mississippi Valley.

The blue catfish is the largest of the catfishes and consistently reached 100 pounds in weight during the nineteenth century, when fish of such dimensions were commonly marketed along the Mississippi River. The largest documented specimen in recent times, from the Osage River in central Missouri, weighed 117 pounds. Captain William Heckman, in his *Steamboating Sixty-five Years on Missouri's Rivers*, re-counted what might have been the grandaddy of all catfishes, a 315-pound blue cat taken in the Missouri River west of Saint Louis. The naturalist Constantine Rafinesque knew of catfishes "weighing 185 pounds and another 250 pounds," undoubtedly big blue catfish. Even Mark Twain lent some credence to the "roaring demon" of the Mississippi River, having seen a "Mississippi catfish that was more than six feet long."

The blue catfish is now uncommon over much of the northern portion of its range, a decline initiated by commercial fishing, the impoundment of the Mississippi River, and the channelization of the Missouri River. The alterations have removed in part the combination of swift runs or "chutes" and deep pools that the species needs in order to flourish. The blue catfish also formerly undertook seasonal migrations in the Mississippi River, moving south into warmer water in the winter and back upstream in summer.

Blue catfish are big game, and the serious angler needs a stout pole and 50-pound test line. The blue cat will congregate below dams in deep holes or swift water, feeding near surface or at the bottom on mussels, fishes, and crayfish. One of the best vantage points for observing blue catfish is immediately below Truman Reservoir in central Missouri. Blue catfish can be caught by the same methods that take channel catfish. Live or cut fish are generally used as bait, with gizzard shad being preferred by experienced anglers for its "scented oil." Anise oil or "licorice scent" is also commonly applied to bait.

Flathead Catfish

Pylodictis olivaris

Plate 89

Colloquial names: yellow cat, shovelhead cat, mud cat, morgan cat, appaloosa cat, Mississippi cat, goujon, bashaw, russian cat, granny cat, pieded cat, flatbelly

Scientific name:
Pylodictis, Greek for "mud fish"
olivaris, Latin for "olive colored"

Distribution: Found throughout much of the central and south-central United States. Most common in reservoirs and large rivers but occasionally found in small streams of the western plains. Introduced west of the Rockies.

Size: Frequently attaining a length of 4 feet and a weight of 50 pounds, to a maximum of about 100 pounds. The world record on hook-and-line weighed 91 lbs. 4 oz. and was caught at the Lewisville Floodgate in Texas in 1982.

Status: Of special concern in North Dakota.

The oversized head and formidable, jutting jaw of the flathead catfish make it a unique, albeit rather repulsive looking catfish. In spite of the widespread prejudice against its looks, the flathead is an important sport fish and commercial food fish. Flatheads are long lived (typically 20 years or more), but they do not grow to be quite as large as the blue catfish. However, the flathead is more common and more widespread than the blue catfish and offers freshwater anglers their best chance at catching a really big fish.

Young flatheads live in riffles and feed principally on immature aquatic insects. Adults are solitary and inhabit deep, sluggish pools, brushpiles, and undercut banks, moving at night into the shallows or the head of the pool to feed. Big flatheads are chiefly piscivorous and do not scavenge like other catfishes. Occasionally a flathead is caught on worms or "stink bait," but knowledgeable river folks bait with live or freshly killed fish. Trot lines, set lines, or jugs are favored techniques when fishing for flatheads. The latter method entails floating live bait from an airtight plastic jug, the buoyancy of which eventually tires a hooked fish and pulls it to the surface.

Flatheads breed in natural cavities of river banks, an instinct that leaves them susceptible to illegal hand fishing or "noodling." Adept noodlers can recognize a big cat's den by feeling the cleanly swept cavity floor and the mound of silt or debris in front of the hole. One may assume that it is the bone-crushing bite of a 60-pound flathead that keeps the slightly squeamish stuck to the bank with rod and reel.

We have kept yearling flatheads in aquaria on a diet of small goldfish (which they seem to eat exclusively at night) and worms. Solitary confinement is the only rule for flatheads, as they will fight with their relatives and eat any other cohabitants in a small aquarium.

The flathead catfish has been widely introduced, sometimes indiscriminately, into Pacific Coast drainages. In the Colorado River in Arizona, the flathead is thought to be contributing to the demise of the endangered Colorado squawfish (a carnivorous minnow that once exceeded weights of 80 pounds) by eating the young (now mostly hatchery transplants) of that species.

Stonecat

Noturus flavus
Plate 90

Colloquial names: madtom, little yellow cat

Scientific name:
Noturus, Greek for "tail over the back"
flavus, Latin for "yellow"

Distribution: Throughout much of the northern United States, from Montana to Maine, south to Tennessee and Oklahoma. Rare in streams of the High Plains.

Size: Commonly 4–6 inches to a maximum of 9 inches. Jordan and Evermann reported "Length, a foot or more" in *American Food and Game Fishes.*

Status: Not threatened in our region. Other madtoms that are threatened in our range include the Neosho madtom (Kansas, Missouri, and Oklahoma) and the Caddo and Ouachita madtoms in Arkansas.

The stonecat is one of the more widely distributed of the madtoms and is the only species large enough to be "regularly" caught on hook-and-line. About 12 species of madtoms occur in our region, most of which are less than 5 inches in length. Rafinesque called this species "yellow backtail" and created for it the genus *Noturus* in reference to the connection between the adipose and tail fins.

The stonecat lives in relatively clear, perennial streams in shallow riffles where it takes refuge by day in the crevices between stones or beneath litter. The stonecat feeds at night on immature insects and occasionally a minnow or darter.

Many catfishes have venom glands at the bases of their pectoral fins, but the toxin is particularly well developed in the madtoms. The madtoms do not inject their toxin in "hypodermic" fashion; instead they release it through pores onto their skin. The pectoral spine is bathed in the venom when the fin is folded against the body, and the skin investing the spine also secretes some venom. A wound from the pectoral spine might be tender and swollen for a week after puncture.

Slender Madtom

Noturus exilis

Plate 91

Colloquial names: madtom, slender stonecat

Scientific name:
Noturus, Greek for "tail over the back"
exilis, Latin for "slim"

Distribution: In our region, largely restricted to clearer streams of Iowa, Missouri, eastern Kansas, eastern Oklahoma, and Arkansas.

Size: Commonly 3–5 inches long, to a maximum of 6 inches.

Status: Protected or of special concern in Minnesota, Mississippi, and Wisconsin.

The slender madtom is similar in most respects to the stonecat but can be discerned by its dark-edged anal and tail fins. The slender madtom is less widely distributed, probably a result in part of its intolerance of silty water. The slender madtom is characteristic of small- to medium-sized streams in the northern Ozarks and some of the clearer creeks and rivers of the tallgrass prairie. In addition to this species and the stonecat, several other kinds of small madtoms inhabit the waters of the central United States, many of which have limited distributions and are protected or of special concern.

Like other madtoms, the slender madtom is an imprecation to careless fishermen for its sharp and toxic spines. Anglers have contrived an excellent bait for smallmouth bass and "goggle-eye" (rock bass) by hooking the madtom through its mouth. But carefully! The madtom's thick skin and slippery coating of mucus make it hard to handle. When held, some species of *Noturus* will rigidly arch their backs, a defensive posture not unlike that of a tomcat—suggestive of the common name madtom!

Madtoms are easily collected from shallow riffles with a seine. The seine is stretched across the downstream end of a riffle, effectively blocking any escape route for the fish, and the stones and debris in the riffle are then kicked or overturned, washing the madtoms and other fishes downstream into the net.

1. Chestnut lamprey, adult, p. 7
   Ichthyomyzon castaneus

2. Immature lamprey (ammocoete), p. 7
   Ichthyomyzon castaneus

3. Lake sturgeon, p. 11
   Acipenser fulvescens

4. Shovelnose sturgeon, p. 12
   Scaphirhynchus platorynchus

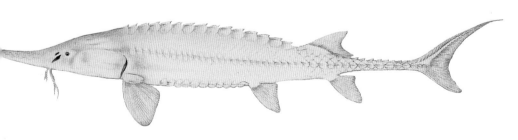

5. Pallid sturgeon, p. 13
   Scaphirhynchus albus

6. Paddlefish, p. 17
Polyodon spathula

7. Alligator gar, p. 21
Lepisosteus spatula

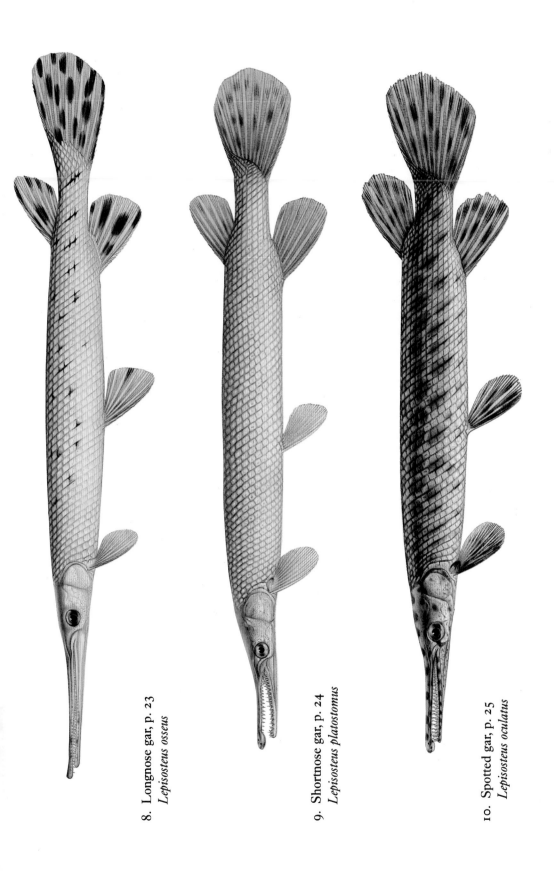

8. Longnose gar, p. 23
Lepisosteus osseus

9. Shortnose gar, p. 24
Lepisosteus platostomus

10. Spotted gar, p. 25
Lepisosteus oculatus

11. Bowfin, adult female, p. 29
    Amia calva

12. Bowfin, juvenile male, p. 29
    Amia calva

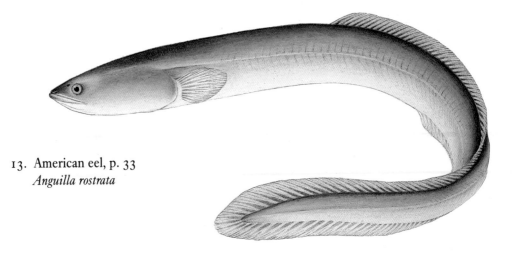

13. American eel, p. 33
    Anguilla rostrata

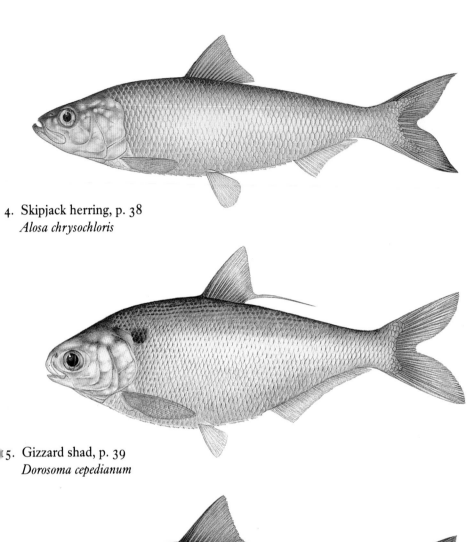

4. Skipjack herring, p. 38
   Alosa chrysochloris

5. Gizzard shad, p. 39
   Dorosoma cepedianum

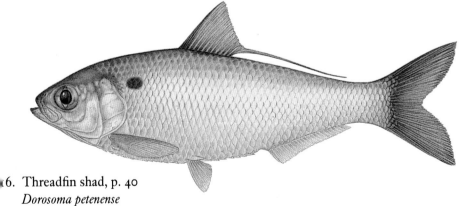

6. Threadfin shad, p. 40
   Dorosoma petenense

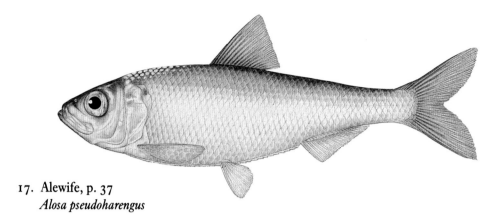

17. Alewife, p. 37
    Alosa pseudoharengus

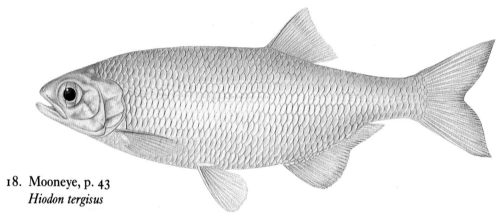

18. Mooneye, p. 43
    Hiodon tergisus

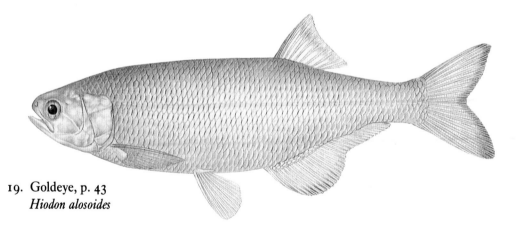

19. Goldeye, p. 43
    Hiodon alosoides

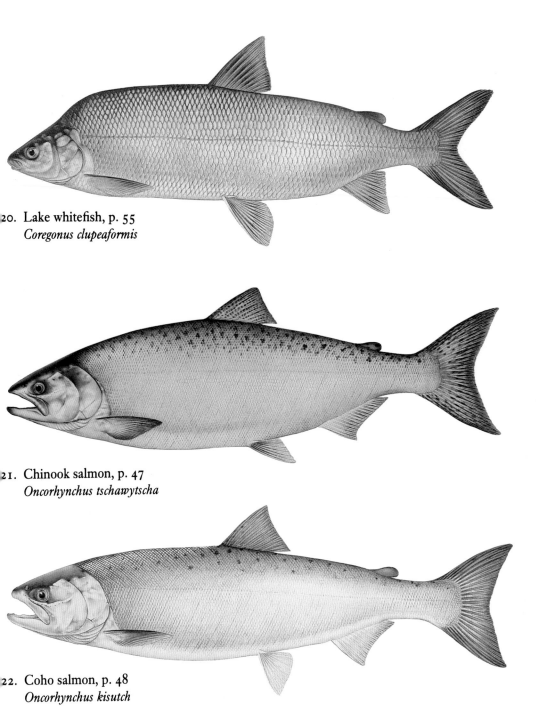

20. Lake whitefish, p. 55
Coregonus clupeaformis

21. Chinook salmon, p. 47
Oncorhynchus tschawytscha

22. Coho salmon, p. 48
Oncorhynchus kisutch

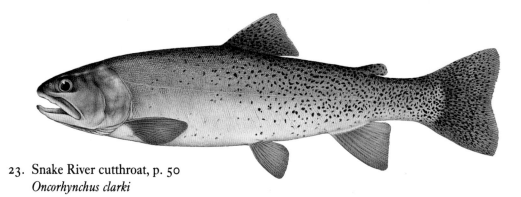

23. Snake River cutthroat, p. 50
    Oncorhynchus clarki

24. Rainbow trout, male, p. 49
    Oncorhynchus mykiss

25. Brown trout, male, p. 52
    Salmo trutta

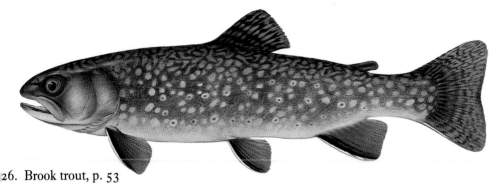

26. Brook trout, p. 53
    Salvelinus fontinalis

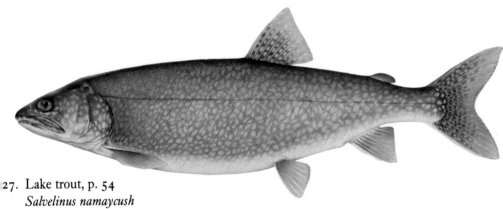

27. Lake trout, p. 54
    Salvelinus namaycush

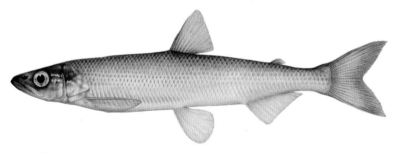

28. Rainbow smelt, p. 59
    Osmerus mordax

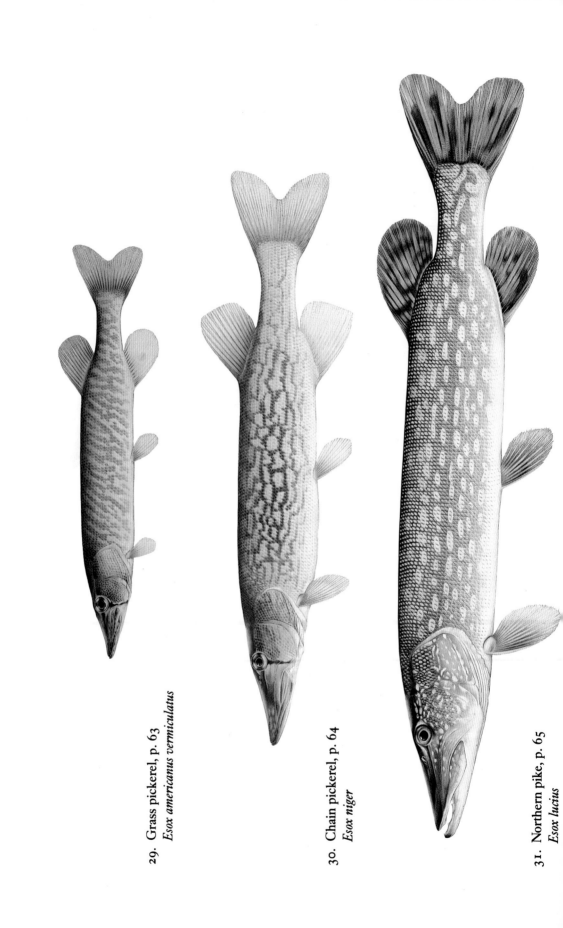

29. Grass pickerel, p. 63
Esox americanus vermiculatus

30. Chain pickerel, p. 64
Esox niger

31. Northern pike, p. 65
Esox lucius

32. Tiger muskie, p. 67
Esox lucius × Esox masquinongy

33. Muskellunge, p. 67
Esox masquinongy

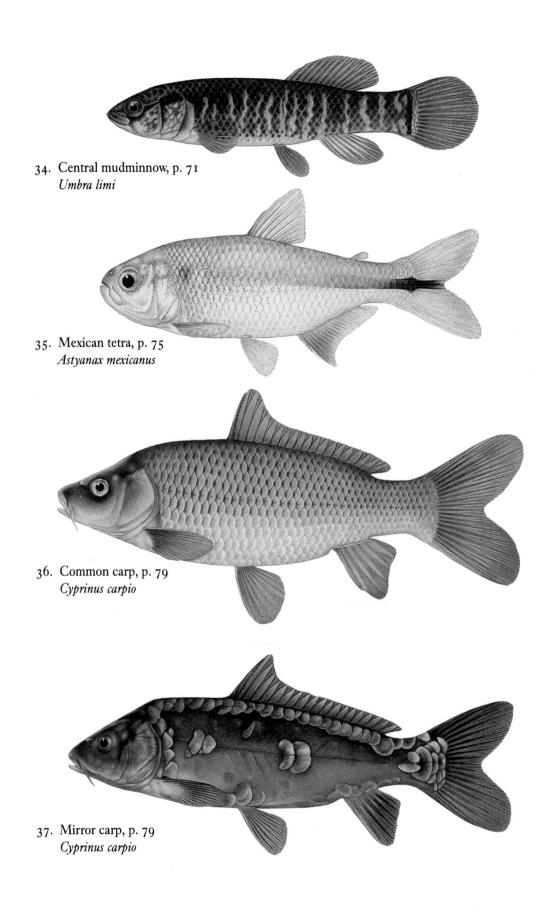

34. Central mudminnow, p. 71
    Umbra limi

35. Mexican tetra, p. 75
    Astyanax mexicanus

36. Common carp, p. 79
    Cyprinus carpio

37. Mirror carp, p. 79
    Cyprinus carpio

38. "Wild" goldfish, p. 81
Carassius auratus

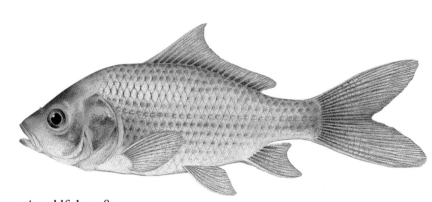

39. Domestic goldfish, p. 81
Carassius auratus

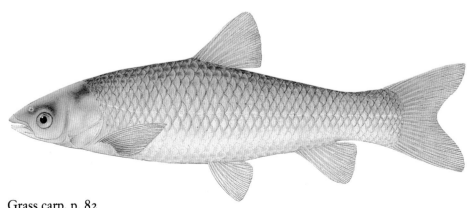

40. Grass carp, p. 82
Ctenopharyngodon idella

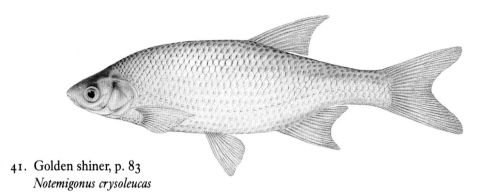

41. Golden shiner, p. 83
    Notemigonus crysoleucas

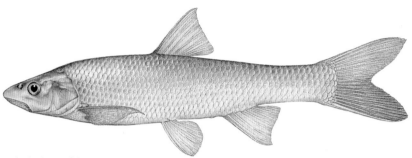

42. Flathead chub, p. 86
    Hybopsis gracilis

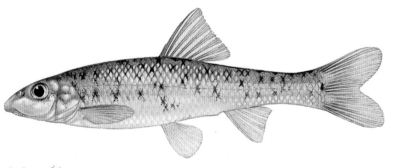

43. Gravel chub, p. 86
    Hybopsis x-punctata

44. Creek chub, p. 84
   Semotilus atromaculatus

45. Redspot chub, post-nuptial male, p. 85
   Nocomis asper

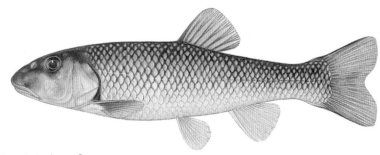

46. Hornyhead chub, p. 85
   Nocomis biguttatus

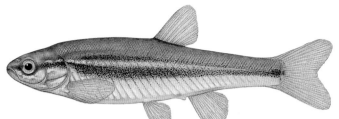

47. Southern redbelly dace, female, p. 87
    Phoxinus erythrogaster

48. Southern redbelly dace, breeding
    male, p. 87
    Phoxinus erythrogaster

49. Blacknose dace, breeding male, p. 88
    Rhinichthys atratulus

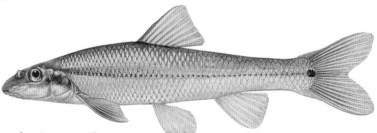

50. Suckermouth minnow, p. 89
    Phenacobius mirabilis

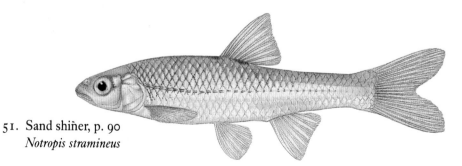

51. Sand shiner, p. 90
    Notropis stramineus

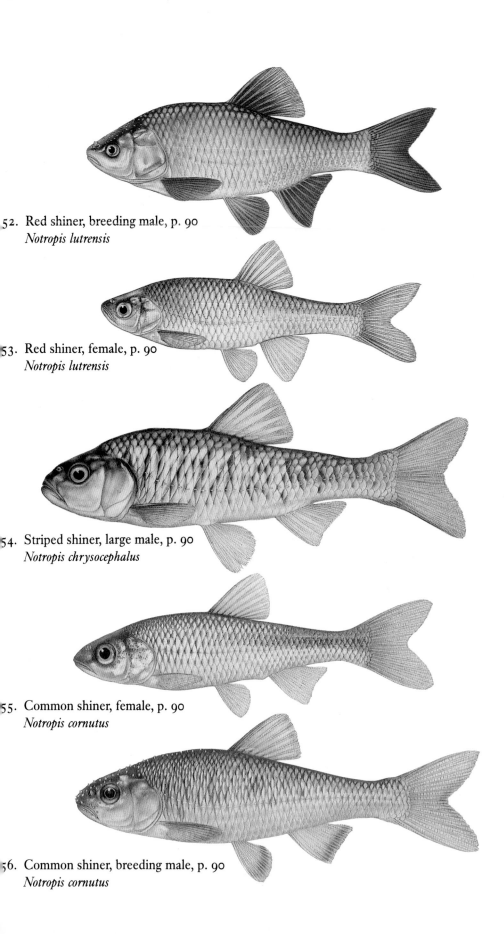

52. Red shiner, breeding male, p. 90
    Notropis lutrensis

53. Red shiner, female, p. 90
    Notropis lutrensis

54. Striped shiner, large male, p. 90
    Notropis chrysocephalus

55. Common shiner, female, p. 90
    Notropis cornutus

56. Common shiner, breeding male, p. 90
    Notropis cornutus

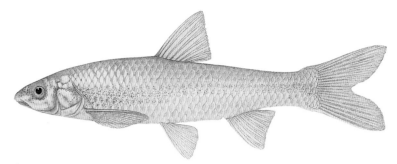

57. Plains minnow, p. 91
    Hybognathus placitus

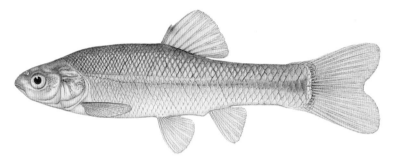

58. Fathead minnow, female, p. 92
    Pimephales promelas

59. Fathead minnow, breeding male, p. 92
    Pimephales promelas

60. Bluntnose minnow, p. 92
    Pimephales notatus

61. Central stoneroller,
    breeding male, p. 93
    Campostoma anomalum

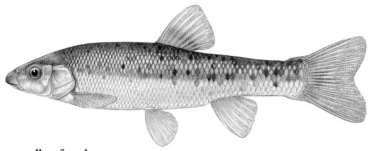

62. Central stoneroller, female, p. 93
    Campostoma anomalum

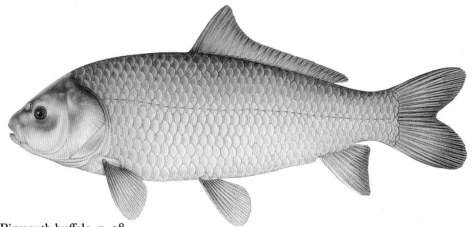

63. Bigmouth buffalo, p. 98
Ictiobus cyprinellus

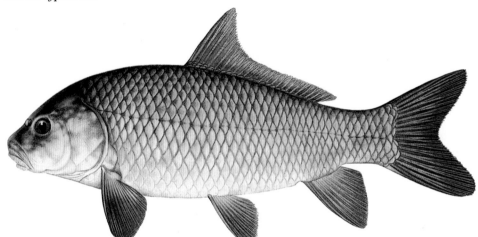

64. Black buffalo, p. 99
Ictiobus niger

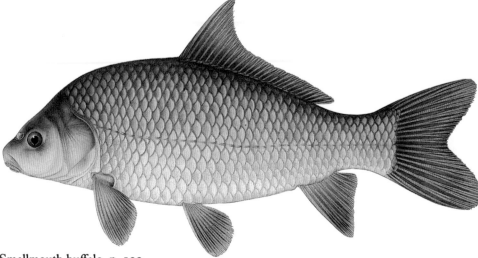

65. Smallmouth buffalo, p. 100
Ictiobus bubalus

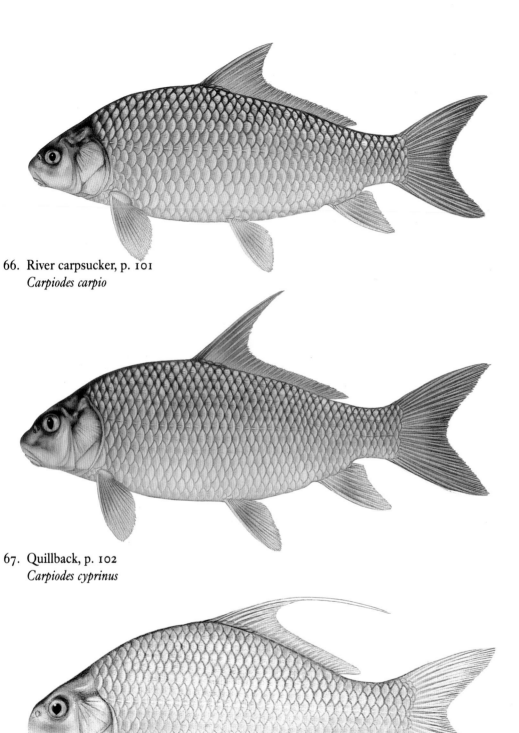

66. River carpsucker, p. 101
    Carpiodes carpio

67. Quillback, p. 102
    Carpiodes cyprinus

68. Highfin carpsucker, p. 103
    Carpiodes velifer

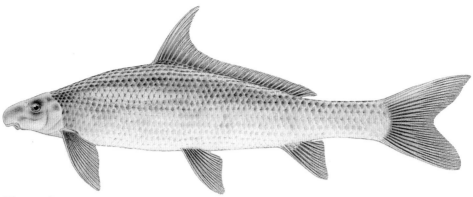

69. Blue sucker, p. 97
Cycleptus elongatus

70. Longnose sucker, p. 104
Catostomus catostomus

71. Mountain sucker, p. 105
Catostomus platyrhynchus

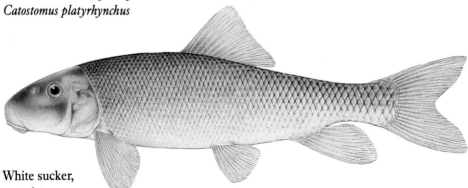

72. White sucker,
p. 106
Catostomus commersoni

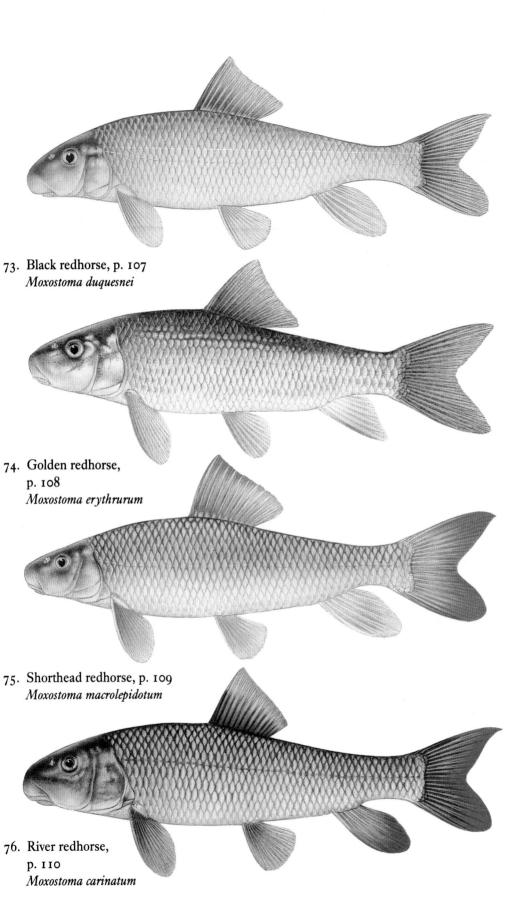

73. Black redhorse, p. 107
Moxostoma duquesnei

74. Golden redhorse,
p. 108
Moxostoma erythrurum

75. Shorthead redhorse, p. 109
Moxostoma macrolepidotum

76. River redhorse,
p. 110
Moxostoma carinatum

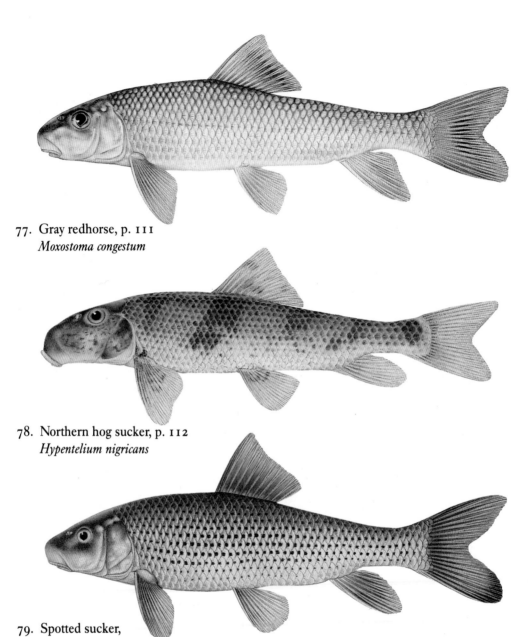

77. Gray redhorse, p. 111
    Moxostoma congestum

78. Northern hog sucker, p. 112
    Hypentelium nigricans

79. Spotted sucker,
    p. 113
    Minytrema melanops

80. Creek chubsucker, p. 114
   Erimyzon oblongus

81. Lake chubsucker, male, p. 114
   Erimyzon sucetta

82. Black bullhead, p. 117
    Ictalurus melas

83. Yellow bullhead, p. 118
    Ictalurus natalis

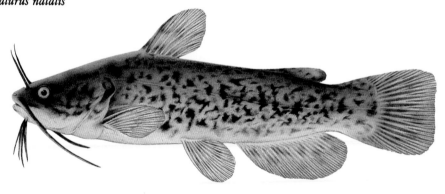

84. Brown bullhead, p. 119
    Ictalurus nebulosus

35. Channel catfish, juvenile, p. 120
   Ictalurus punctatus

36. Channel catfish, 2 lb. adult, p. 120
   Ictalurus punctatus

37. Channel catfish, breeding male, p. 120
   Ictalurus punctatus

88. Blue catfish, p. 122
   Ictalurus furcatus

89. Flathead catfish, p. 123
   Pylodictis olivaris

90. Stonecat, p. 124
   Noturus flavus

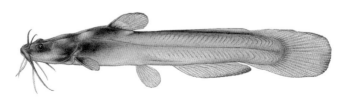

91. Slender madtom, p. 125
   Noturus exilis

92. Trout-perch, p. 129
    Percopsis omiscomaycus

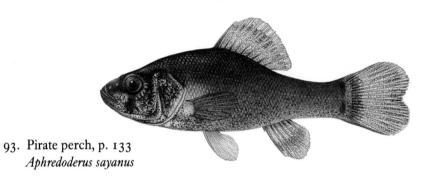

93. Pirate perch, p. 133
    Aphredoderus sayanus

94. Burbot, p. 137
    Lota lota

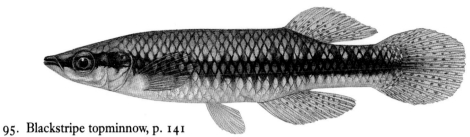

95. Blackstripe topminnow, p. 141
   Fundulus notatus

96. Northern studfish, p. 141
   Fundulus catenatus

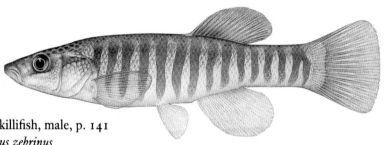

97. Plains killifish, male, p. 141
   Fundulus zebrinus

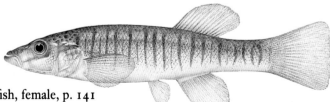

98. Plains killifish, female, p. 141
   Fundulus zebrinus

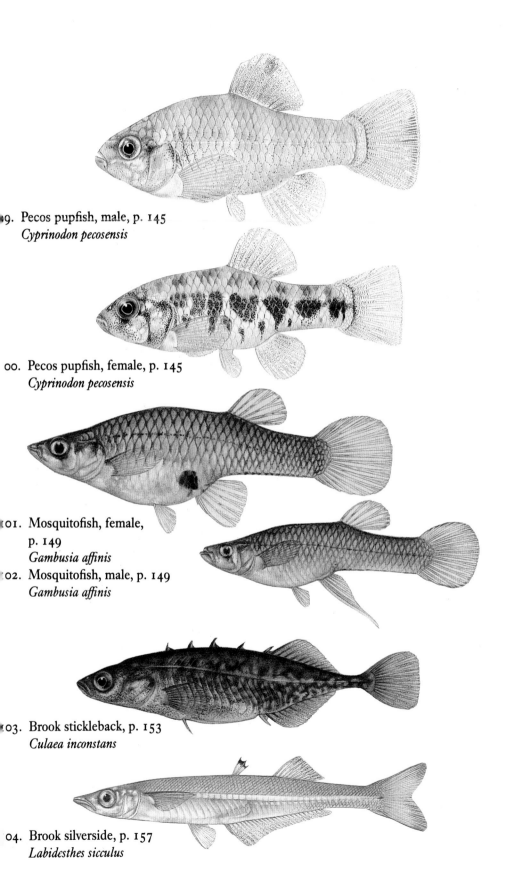

99. Pecos pupfish, male, p. 145
   Cyprinodon pecosensis

00. Pecos pupfish, female, p. 145
   Cyprinodon pecosensis

01. Mosquitofish, female,
   p. 149
   Gambusia affinis

02. Mosquitofish, male, p. 149
   Gambusia affinis

03. Brook stickleback, p. 153
   Culaea inconstans

04. Brook silverside, p. 157
   Labidesthes sicculus

105. Striped bass, p. 161
Morone saxatilis

106. White bass, p. 163
Morone chrysops

107. Wiper, p. 164
Morone saxatilis × Morone chrysops

108. Yellow bass, female, p. 165
Morone mississippiensis

109. Yellow bass,
breeding male, p. 165
Morone mississippiensis

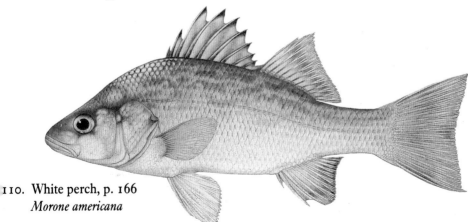

110. White perch, p. 166
Morone americana

111. Northern largemouth
bass, p. 169
Micropterus salmoides salmoides

112. Florida largemouth
bass, p. 169
Micropterus salmoides floridanus

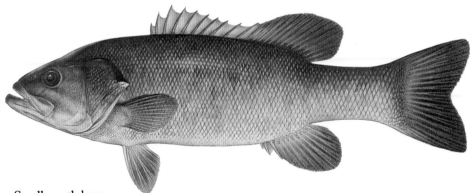

113. Smallmouth bass,
color variation, p. 171
Micropterus dolomieui

114. Northern spotted bass,
p. 173
Micropterus punctulatus punctulatus

115. Northern smallmouth
bass, p. 171
Micropterus dolomieui dolomieui

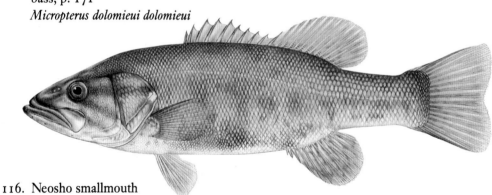

116. Neosho smallmouth
bass, p. 171
Micropterus dolomieui velox

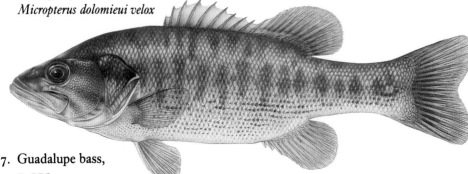

117. Guadalupe bass,
p. 175
Micropterus treculi

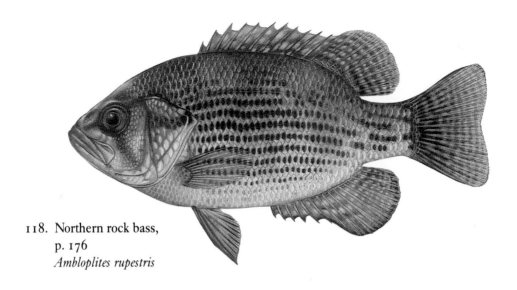

118. Northern rock bass,
p. 176
Ambloplites rupestris

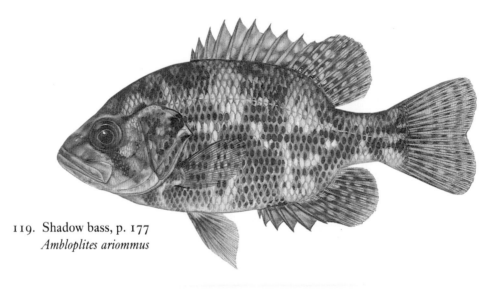

119. Shadow bass, p. 177
Ambloplites ariommus

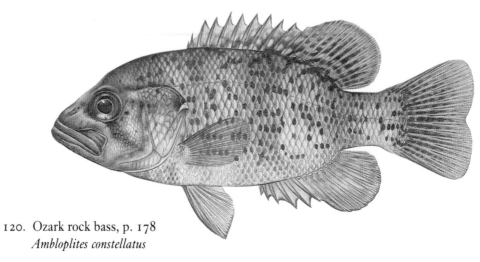

120. Ozark rock bass, p. 178
Ambloplites constellatus

121. Warmouth, from
Mingo Swamp, Missouri, p. 179
Chaenobryttus gulosus

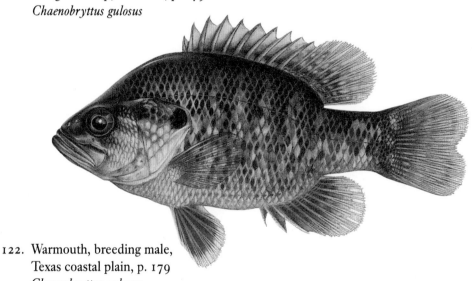

122. Warmouth, breeding male,
Texas coastal plain, p. 179
Chaenobryttus gulosus

123. Warmouth, female,
Texas coastal plain, p. 179
Chaenobryttus gulosus

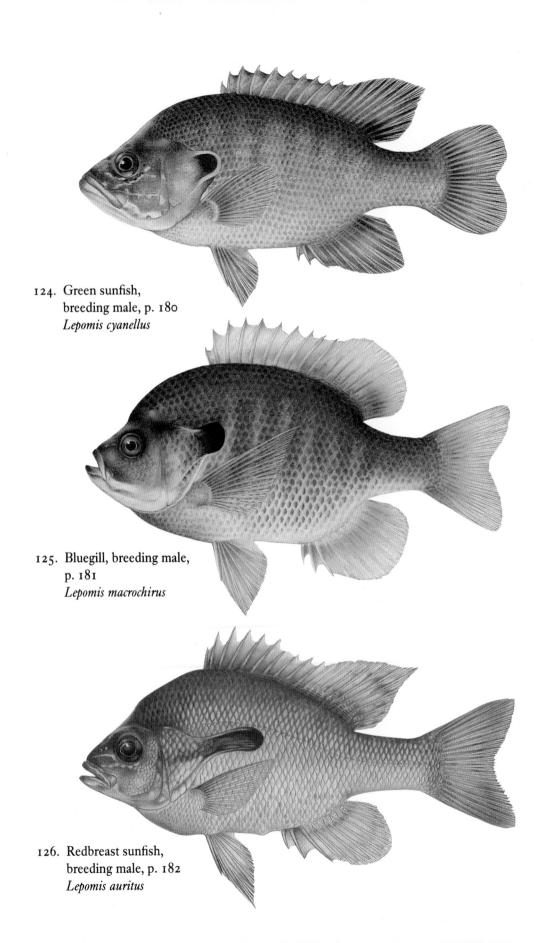

124. Green sunfish,
     breeding male, p. 180
     Lepomis cyanellus

125. Bluegill, breeding male,
     p. 181
     Lepomis macrochirus

126. Redbreast sunfish,
     breeding male, p. 182
     Lepomis auritus

127. Green sunfish, juvenile,
p. 180
Lepomis cyanellus

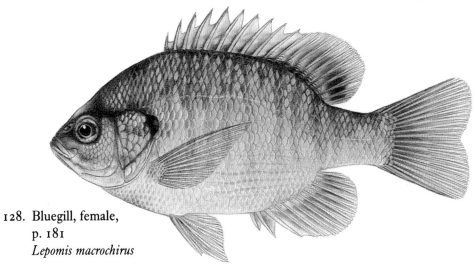

128. Bluegill, female,
p. 181
Lepomis macrochirus

129. Redbreast sunfish, female,
p. 182
Lepomis auritus

130. Redear sunfish, breeding male,
    p. 183
    Lepomis microlophus

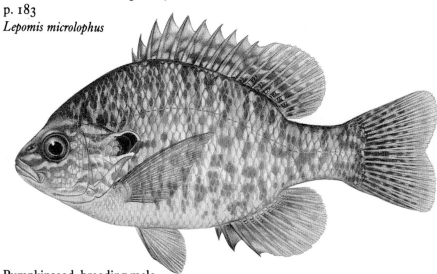

131. Pumpkinseed, breeding male,
    p. 184
    Lepomis gibbosus

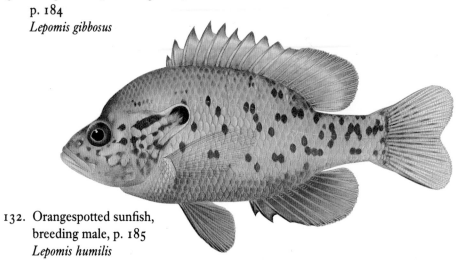

132. Orangespotted sunfish,
    breeding male, p. 185
    Lepomis humilis

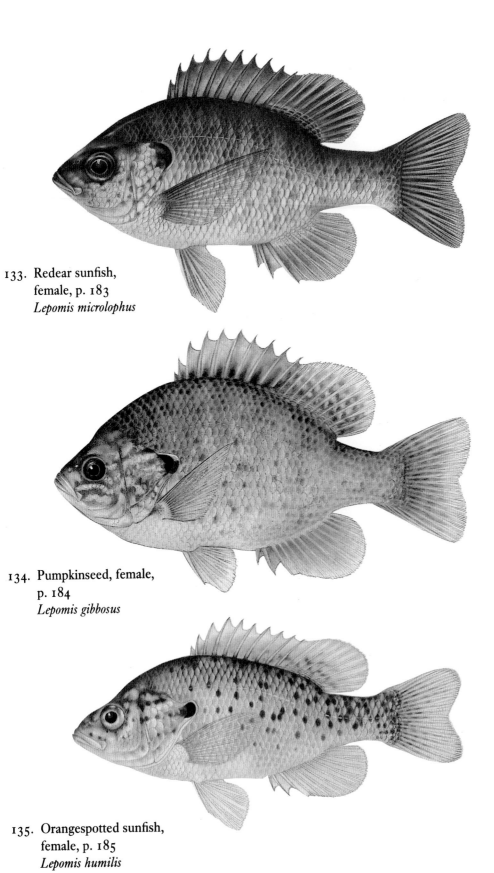

133. Redear sunfish,
     female, p. 183
     Lepomis microlophus

134. Pumpkinseed, female,
     p. 184
     Lepomis gibbosus

135. Orangespotted sunfish,
     female, p. 185
     Lepomis humilis

136. Spotted sunfish, breeding male,
    p. 186
    Lepomis punctatus miniatus

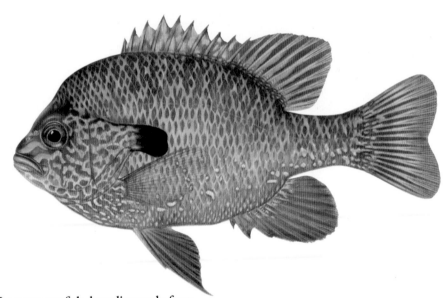

137. Longear sunfish, breeding male from
    North Fork River, Missouri, p. 187
    Lepomis megalotis

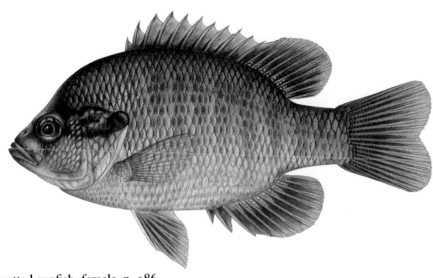

138. Spotted sunfish, female, p. 186
    Lepomis punctatus miniatus

139. Longear sunfish, female from Osage
    drainage, Missouri, p. 187
    Lepomis megalotis

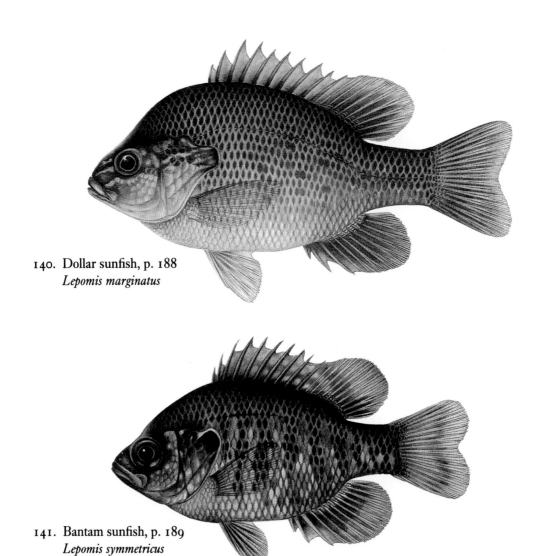

140. Dollar sunfish, p. 188
Lepomis marginatus

141. Bantam sunfish, p. 189
Lepomis symmetricus

142. Orangespotted sunfish × bluegill,
     male, p. 190

143. Bluegill × green sunfish,
     male, p. 190

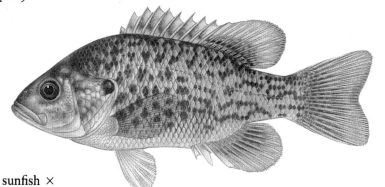

144. Green sunfish ×
     orangespotted sunfish, p. 190

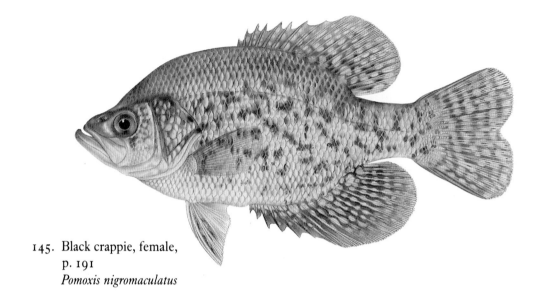

145. Black crappie, female,
p. 191
Pomoxis nigromaculatus

146. Black crappie, breeding male, p. 191
Pomoxis nigromaculatus

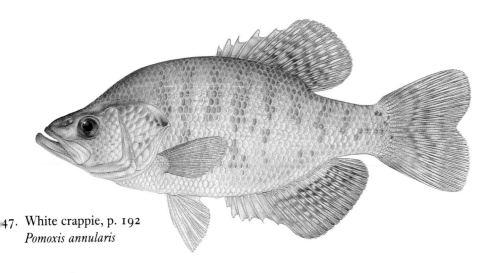

47. White crappie, p. 192
Pomoxis annularis

48. Flier, p. 193
Centrarchus macropterus

149. Walleye, p. 197
Stizostedion vitreum

150. Sauger, p. 199
Stizostedion canadense

151. Yellow perch, p. 200
Perca flavescens

152. Logperch, p. 201
Percina caprodes

153. Slenderhead darter,
breeding male, p. 201
Percina phoxocephala

154. Johnny darter, p. 202
Etheostoma nigrum

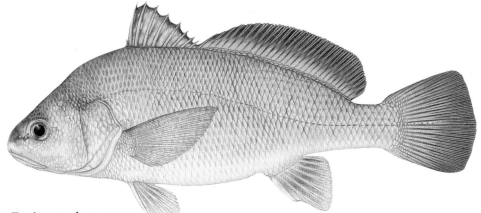

161. Freshwater drum, p. 207
Aplodinotus grunniens

162. Rio Grande perch, p. 211
Cichlasoma cyanoguttatum

163. Ozark sculpin, p. 215
Cottus hypselurus

Trout-Perches

Family PERCOPSIDAE

Like,—but oh how different.
—William Wordsworth
    Yes, It Was the Mountain Echo

Trout-Perch

Percopsis omiscomaycus

Plate 92

Colloquial names: sand roller, grounder minnow

Scientific name:
Percopsis, Greek for "perch-like"
omiscomaycus, Algonquian Indian word with "trout" as its root

Distribution: Alaska, much of Canada, and the northern United States, south to Missouri and Maryland. In our range, mostly in northern Iowa, North Dakota, and Minnesota and occurring in a few prairie streams in central Missouri.

Size: Usually 3–5 inches.

Status: Protected in South Dakota and of special concern in Montana and Missouri.

Although it's neither trout nor perch, the trout-perch has characteristics of both soft-rayed and spiny-rayed fishes and is thought to be a transitional remnant between the two groups. Along with its relatives, the sand roller, the pirate perch, and the cave-fishes, the trout-perch is a holdover from an ancient group of fishes that once inhabited the Mississippi River valley.

Trout-perches live in lakes and in sandy or gravelly streams with a permanent flow of relatively clear water. The trout-perch is a nocturnal species, hiding on the bottom among litter and submerged objects during the day and moving into shallow water at night to feed on aquatic invertebrates. Trout-perch typically spawn over sand or gravel in the shallow riffles of streams or along sandy or gravelly shorelines of lakes.

Where abundant in the northern part of its range (particularly in glacial lakes), the trout-perch is an important forage fish for walleye, northern pike, and other sport fishes. The trout-perch is becoming less common along the southern and western fringes of its distribution, probably because of the increased turbidity in streams.

Pirate Perches

Family APHREDODERIDAE

You are an odd fish.
—Langdon Mitchell
  The New York Idea

Pirate Perch

Aphredoderus sayanus

Plate 93

Colloquial names: pirate, mud perch

Scientific name:
Aphredoderus, Greek *aphod* for "excrement" and Greek *dere* for "throat," in reference to the unusual position of the anus—properly *"Aphododerus"*
sayanus, for Thomas Say, an entomologist, and Latin *anus,* again referring to the position of the anus

Distribution: Chiefly in the Mississippi River valley and along the southern Atlantic and Gulf coasts. Coming into our region in Mingo Swamp (southeast Missouri), southern and eastern Arkansas, east Texas, and Louisiana.

Size: Adults range from 2 to 5 inches.

Status: The pirate perch is protected or of special concern in Iowa, Ohio, and Wisconsin.

The pirate perch is the only living member of its family. An unusual feature of this species is that the anus is located in the normal position near the anal fin in young fish but moves forward toward the throat as the fish grows and matures—a rearrangement that proffers an alternative derivation of the odd scientific epithet *"say" anus.*

The pirate perch inhabits swamps, lowland lakes, and quiet backwaters of low gradient streams, preferring clear, warm water with little or no current and abundant aquatic vegetation or debris for cover. Solitary and nocturnal, pirate perch hide among the vegetation or other structure during the day and forage along the bottom for invertebrates and small minnows at night. The pirate perch is tolerant of high water temperatures and low oxygen, as are most swamp fishes, and its common associates include such swamp denizens as the bantam sunfish, spotted gar, banded pygmy sunfish, warmouth, flier, bullheads, and bowfin. Pirate perch are not known to build nests, and they probably incubate their eggs in their mouths, as do the cavefishes.

The name of *pirate* was coined by the famous naturalist, Charles C. Abbott, M.D., in 1866, for the species' greedy, carnivorous habits in the aquarium. Pirate perch are probably of little economic importance, but in a pinch they have served us well as bait for chain pickerel. The pirate perch is declining in some regions as a result of lowland drainage.

Codfishes

Family GADIDAE

Of all the fish that swim or swish
  in ocean's deep autocracy,
There's none possess such haughtiness,
  as the codfish aristocracy.
—*Wallace Irwin*
  Codfish Aristocracy

Burbot

Lota lota

Plate 94

Colloquial names: ling, freshwater cod, lawyer, spineless cat, eelpout, dogfish, mother eel, cusk, sand ling

Scientific name:
Lota, from the French *la lotte* for "cod"

Distribution: Throughout Alaska and Canada. In our range principally a northern species, occurring in the Missouri and upper Mississippi rivers. Also found in the northeastern United States, northwest Wyoming, and much of western Montana.

Size: Commonly growing to 5 pounds. The world record weighed 18 lbs. 4 oz.

Status: Protected or of special concern in several states, including Iowa and Missouri. Sport fish in Wyoming and other states.

The codfish family is represented by 25 species in North America, including such famous food fishes as the cod and haddock. The burbot is the only member of the codfish family restricted to inland waters; it inhabits the colder waters of northern North America, Asia, and Europe. The slender body, long dorsal and anal fins, and the single barbel on its chin give the burbot a distinctive "snaky" look and a superficial resemblance to the eel and the catfish—hence the common vernacular of eelpout.

The burbot is widely known as lawyer, a nickname applied for its gluttonous feeding and its aggressive habit of "biting at anything." As a consequence, the burbot's stomach is sometimes grossly distended with crayfish, invertebrates, and fish. The burbot prefers the deeper, cooler waters of lakes and large rivers, normally hiding among the bottom structures during the day and emerging at night to feed.

Unlike most other fishes, the burbot spawns in winter. Spawning occurs at night, typically under the cover of ice in shallow sandy bays or gravel shoals. Burbots do not build nests and give no parental care to their young.

In many parts of North America, the burbot is cursed as a trash fish that harms the sport fishery; and for most anglers the burbot has no utility except as an occasional meal for herring gulls or tomcats. Despite widespread prejudices against the burbot, the species serves to regulate populations of other fishes. In some Scandinavian countries, the burbot's large liver is sold smoked or canned and, like cod liver oil, is a valuable source of vitamin D.

Killifishes and Topminnows

Family FUNDULIDAE

When the bait is worth more than the catch, 'tis
time to stop fishing.
—Angler's proverb

Killifishes and Topminnows

Fundulus spp.

Plates 95–98

Scientific name:
Fundulus, Latin from *fundus* for "bottom," a peculiar name for a topminnow but originally coined for a bottom species of the Atlantic Coast, being "the abode of the 'fundulus mudfish.'"

Distribution: Principally east of the Rocky Mountains, except for the California killifish.

Size: Normally about 1.5–4 inches, but the northern studfish reaches 6 inches in length.

Status: Several species are protected or of special concern in states near the margins of their ranges.

The killifish family includes members of five genera and has about 40 species native to North America and the Caribbean islands. Members of the genus *Fundulus* go by the common names of killifish, studfish, and topminnow. About six of the 25 fishes of this genus occur in the central United States, the most widespread being the plains killifish, plains topminnow, and blackstripe topminnow.

The topminnows and killifishes are typically found near shores of streams, in the backwaters, or in runs of small- to moderate-sized streams. Several species prefer water with dense vegetation. All species of *Fundulus* have an upturned, terminal mouth, which is an adaptation for feeding at the surface, although the plains killifish and northern studfish sometimes feed off the bottom. Spawning behavior varies among the species, but none of the topminnows build nests or provide direct parental protection for the eggs and young. Blackstripe topminnows defend territories as a pair and deposit their eggs on submerged plants or algae. The males of the northern studfish (pictured) develop intense breeding colors and establish small territories. The female studfish deposits her eggs on clean gravel. Plains killifish establish no territories, but the males will fight among themselves. Killifish bury their eggs in the sand.

The northern studfish is characteristic of the clear Ozark streams of Arkansas and Missouri, where it is the most abundant topminnow. When being pursued or otherwise disturbed, it has the rather ridiculous habit of flip-flopping itself across the surface of the water, until satisfied that safer shallows have been reached. The plains killifish, known colloquially as zebra, tiger, or penitentiary minnow, is commonly found in sandy, saline creeks and rivers of the High Plains. The blackstripe topminnow inhabits pools and slow-moving rivers in the Mississippi Valley and is fairly common in southeast Kansas, eastern Oklahoma and eastern Texas. Both plains killifish and northern studfish can be caught on hook-and-line, but they are too small to eat and, as the old adage suggests, are probably worth less than the bait.

The name *killifish* is derived from the Dutch word *kill,* meaning a small creek or drainage, where the species is typically found. *Kill* is used in the northeastern United States as a reference to creeks or other waterways, as in Schuylkill River (in Philadelphia) and Catskill Mountains (southeastern New York).

Pupfishes

Family CYPRINODONTIDAE

If you were to make little fishes talk, they would
talk like whales.
—Oliver Goldsmith, quoted in
   Boswell's Life of Dr. Johnson

Pecos Pupfish and Red River Pupfish

Cyprinodon pecosensis and *Cyprinodon rubrofluviatilis*

Plates 99–100

Colloquial names: alkali minnow, pursy minnow

Scientific name:
Cyprinodon, Greek from *cyprino* for "carp" and Latin from *dent* meaning "tooth"; not related to the carp, but so named because they differ from the minnows by having the jaws more projecting and toothed
pecosensis, "of the Pecos River"
rubrofluviatilis, Latin for "red river"

Distribution: Pecos pupfish occurs in that drainage in New Mexico and Texas; the Red River pupfish occupies the upper Red River drainage of Oklahoma and Texas.

Size: Usually about 1–1.5 inches.

Status: Because of extremely limited distributions, most species of *Cyprinodon* are protected or of special concern, except the Red River pupfish and a widely distributed coastal species, the sheepshead minnow.

The New World cyprinodonts occur in North America and throughout the Caribbean islands in brackish and freshwater habitats, but they are most noted for their success in extreme environments. In North America, they are often the only fishes found in waters of high temperatures, high conductivity and alkalinity, and excessive concentrations of other chemicals characteristic of desert springs. About 30 species of pupfishes in the genus *Cyprinodon* live in Mexican deserts or the southwestern United States. The Red River and Pecos pupfish are the most widely distributed species within our geographic area. The

common name pupfish was coined by Dr. Carl Hubbs, who thought their aggressive behavior reminiscent of playful puppies.

The Pecos pupfish is found in the Pecos River valley of New Mexico and Texas in saline springs, gypsum sinkholes, and small streams that have a high salt content. The Red River pupfish is native to the headwater reaches of the Red and Brazos rivers of Oklahoma and Texas in clear, shallow, somewhat saline waters. Pupfishes eat invertebrates, bits of plants, and diatoms or other types of algae, feeding both at the water surface and on the bottom. Individuals of some species of pupfishes excavate depressions in the soft bottom substrate, presumably in search of food, and will aggressively defend them from intruders. The male Pecos pupfish turns a bright, metallic blue during spawning and, as do other pupfishes, establishes and defends its territory during its long breeding season. Eggs are deposited on firm substrates or submerged plants.

Some species of pupfishes in the desert southwest and Texas are endemic to a single spring, drainage, or water hole and are usually the only species of fish in that particular body of water. The phenomenon is reflected in their common names: Leon Springs pupfish, White River pupfish, Devil's Hole pupfish, and so on. Their limited distributions put many of these species of pupfishes in imminent danger of extinction because of potential groundwater declines, introductions of predators (e.g., green sunfish), introductions of competitors (e.g., mosquitofish), or other perturbations. Consequently, some pupfishes have a federal listing as endangered or threatened species.

Livebearers

Family POECILIIDAE

*In reservoirs in the southern part of Central
Asia, the fish competes for food with various
carps, particularly with the wild carp . . . as a
result of the introduction of the mosquitofish
into carp ponds, the fertility of the former
decreases sharply, while the growth of the latter
is retarded.*
—*G. V. Nikol'skii*
Special Ichthyology

Mosquitofish and Gambusias

Gambusia spp.

Plates 101–102

Colloquial names: guppy (the true guppy is *Poecilia reticulata*)

Scientific name:
Gambusia, from the Cuban *gambusino* (explained below)

Distribution: Most species have a limited distribution within the area from southeastern New Mexico through south-central Texas, except the mosquitofish, which is native to the northeastern coast of Mexico and the southeastern United States from New Mexico to Illinois to Delaware. Also introduced in other parts of the world.

Size: Mosquitofish males 0.75–1.5 inches; females 1.25–2.25 inches.

Status: The mosquitofish is not threatened in any state, but some gambusias in New Mexico and Texas are rare and very similar in appearance; thus, all gambusias in these states are protected.

The livebearer family comprises fishes that give birth to living young. Among them are several species familiar to freshwater aquarists: guppy, swordtails, and mollies. Sexual dimorphism is pronounced in many species. The males are often the smaller sex, and their anal fins are modified with elongated, tubular rays for the transfer of sperm, making these fishes unusual for their internal fertilization. The most widespread abundant representative of this family in the central United States is the mos-

quitofish (*Gambusia affinis*). Six other species of federally threatened or endangered *Gambusia* occur in a handful of localities in New Mexico and Texas. Although most of our livebearers live in the warmth of southern North America, several species, including green swordtails and mosquitofish, have been introduced by aquarists into hot springs as far north as Alberta, Canada. The origin of the name *Gambusia* is credited to the Cuban naturalist, Felipe Poey. Jordan and Evermann, in *Fishes of North and Middle America,* quote Poey's explanation: "The name owes its etymology to the provincial Cuban word *Gambusino* which signifies nothing, with the idea of a joke or a farce. Thus one says 'to fish for *Gambusinos*' when one catches nothing."

The breeding season of the mosquitofish lasts from two to four months. The female stores sperm in a special pouch and is consequently capable of fertilizing several broods during one season from a single mating. A brood contains up to 100 fish, and those born early in the season can usually reproduce that same summer.

Mosquitofish live principally in vegetated backwater pools within the top few inches of the water's surface. The species is omnivorous and eats whatever food is most readily available. In the past, mosquitofish were routinely and indiscriminately introduced for mosquito control. In hindsight, most native fishes are probably just as effective at controlling mosquito larvae; *mosquitofish* is simply a more marketable denomination.

Sticklebacks

Family GASTEROSTEIDAE

*The differences are manifest. The carp is large
and placid, the stickleback small, slim,
turbulent and fidgety.*
—*Louis Roule*
   "The Carp and the Stickleback" in
   Fishes and Their Ways of Life

Brook Stickleback

Culaea inconstans

Plate 103

Colloquial names: five-spined stickleback, six-spined stickleback, variable stickleback, black stickleback, common stickleback, pinfish

Scientific name:
Culaea, coined from the former generic name *Eucalia,* Greek for "good nest" *inconstans,* Latin for "variable"

Distribution: Northwest Territories and British Columbia to Nova Scotia, south through the Great Lakes region to Iowa, Nebraska, and Montana. Relict populations in northeastern New Mexico.

Size: About 1.5–3.5 inches.

Status: Protected in Nebraska and New Mexico.

The six species of sticklebacks in North America are represented in the north-central United States by the brook stickleback, which occurs as far south as Nebraska and Iowa. Although an isolated population in northeastern New Mexico might have been introduced, it is believed to persist from a more widespread southern range in glacial times. Found in the northern and coastal regions of North America, Europe, and Asia, sticklebacks are named for their well-developed, isolated dorsal spines. Most sticklebacks have smooth and scaleless bodies, but some species, including the brook stickleback, have bony plates along their lateral lines.

Brook sticklebacks inhabit cold, clear to slightly turbid streams, spring-fed ponds, and the shallow edges of lakes. Sticklebacks live in and around dense aquatic vegetation, often in very shallow, marshy seepage water, but Mother Nature sometimes surprises them. In *The Fishes of Alberta,* Paetz and Nelson remarked that "tornado-rain storms in Alberta have been known to deposit this fish in large numbers in farmers [*sic*] fields." Sticklebacks are mostly carnivorous, eating mosquito larvae, other invertebrates, and lesser amounts of fish eggs and algae.

In spring, the male brook stickleback builds a globular nest of dead grass, filamentous algae, and other plant materials, which he binds together with a "waterproof glue" that is secreted from his kidneys and associated organs. The nests are usually built around and securely attached to a plant stem. Initially the nest has a single opening, but after the male coaxes a female into the nest and she deposits her eggs, she breaks out through the back of the nest, creating a second hole that is promptly repaired by the male. The male will then fertilize the eggs and swim back outside to pugnaciously defend his territory. The male stickleback will typically position himself in front of the nest entrance where he can aerate the eggs by fanning his pectoral fins. The male remains vigilant after the eggs hatch and retrieves in his mouth any larvae that stray from the nest. Within several days, the young escape the nest faster than the male can return them. The male then either abandons the nest or solves the problem by eating the remaining fry.

Silversides

Family ATHERINIDAE

No high ambition may I claim—
I angle not for lordly game
Of trout or bass, or weary bream—
A black perch reaches the extreme
Of my desires; and goggle-eyes
Are not a thing that I despise;
A sunfish, or a "chub," or "cat"—
A "silverside"—yea, even that!
—James Whitcomb Riley
   At Broad Ripple

Brook Silverside

Labidesthes sicculus

Plate 104

Colloquial names: skipjack, glassfish, topwater

Scientific name:
Labidesthes, Greek from *labidos* for "pair of forceps" and *esthio*, "to eat" (a reference to the shape of the mouth)
sicculus, Latin for "dried," a reference to the shallow, drying pools in which the species is sometimes found

Distribution: Mississippi River and southern Great Lakes drainages; other Gulf and Atlantic coast drainages from eastern Texas to South Carolina. Absent from the Dakotas, Nebraska, and the southern High Plains.

Size: From 2.5 to 4 inches.

Status: Not threatened in any state.

Most of the approximately 170 species of silversides found around the world are marine, including the famous California grunion, a species well known for its spectacular spawning "runs" on sandy beaches. Only two of the 12 species in the United States and Canada occur very far inland: the brook silverside and tidewater silverside. Silversides were once known as *pescados del rey,* or "fishes of the king," because of the fine eating afforded by many of the saltwater species. The name of silverside is derived from the bright silvery stripe along each side of this sparsely pigmented, nearly transparent fish.

Inland populations of the tidewater silverside, *Menidia beryllina* (formerly known as the Mississippi silverside, *Menidia audens*), live in larger rivers and reservoirs in the southeastern portion of the central United States. Our most widespread and abundant species is the brook silverside. It occurs in clear, warm waters of stream pools or overflows and is the most common "little fish" in the coves and along the shores of Ozark reservoirs. Brook silversides travel in schools and typically live their entire lives within 6 inches of the water's surface, making themselves easy prey for both birds and fishes. Silversides feed on a variety of invertebrates.

Brook silversides are positively phototropic (attracted to light), and shining a light can attract large schools of these fish at night. Bright, moonlit nights will bring about a flurry of activity from the silversides as described by A. R. Cahn: "The silversides seem to go crazy, as if they were moon-struck. They dart about at a most startling speed, dashing here and there, leaping out of the water again and again, bumping into each other, splashing, circling, behaving in a most exaggerated manner. . . ."

Brook silversides spawn once and seldom live longer than a year and one-half. They are not hardy enough to make a good bait, but they are an important forage species for many sport fishes, birds, and other animals.

Temperate Basses

Family PERCICHTHYIDAE

Only the gamefish swims upstream, but the
sensible fish swims down.
—Ogden Nash
  When You Say That, Smile

The temperate basses include the true freshwater basses and several of their anadromous cousins. The temperate basses have only recently been separated from the Serranidae, a large and diverse family of sea basses that includes such familiar fishes as the giant jewfishes and the groupers. The temperate basses are represented in our region by four species and one artificially propagated hybrid. Two species, the white and yellow basses, are native to the central United States and are strictly freshwater fishes. The other two—the white perch and striped bass—are by nature anadromous but can live their entire lives in fresh water and have been transplanted to inland reservoirs and lakes.

Our temperate basses are pelagic fishes, often schooling in water far from shore, where they feed principally upon small, schooling fish. The young of the freshwater species feed primarily upon tiny free-floating crustaceans.

During spring, the freshwater basses make spawning runs in large schools from open lake water into tributary streams or from large rivers into lesser tributaries. Mature white bass will migrate as two separate groups, the males leaving for the spawning grounds about a month before the females. Eggs and milt are released over a gravelly run or riffle, and the fertilized eggs settle and adhere to the bottom of the river where they hatch in a few days. The temperate basses do not build nests, and the parent fish abandon the fertilized eggs. The female white bass compensates for the lack of nurture with an exceptional fecundity, depositing from 250,000 to 900,000 eggs; thus, the white bass has tremendous reproductive potential and no limits are usually placed on its harvest. The temperate basses are valuable sport fishes and are widely known for their spectacular spring spawning runs, when they are most vulnerable to anglers.

Striped Bass

Morone saxatilis

Plate 105

Colloquial names: striper, rockfish, rock, greenhead, squid hound

Scientific name:
Morone, of unknown derivation
saxatilis, Latin for "rock inhabiting"

Distribution: Found along the Atlantic and Gulf coasts; introduced successfully on the Pacific Coast. Stocked into many reservoirs in the southern and central United States.

Size: From 20–50 pounds in freshwater impoundments. Saltwater fish average slightly larger. Ninety- to 100-pound fish were occasionally netted by commercial fishermen in the nineteenth century, the largest being a 125-pound fish from North Carolina in 1891. The world record land-locked striper is 66 lbs. from the O'Neill Forebay in California in 1988.

Status: Introduced into our region. Threatened in some coastal states.

Few fishes present the combination of fine eating and excellent sport that is offered by the striped bass. The rockfish earned its reputation in the nineteenth century when it was abundant and exceptionally popular among commercial fishermen and anglers along the East Coast. Jordan and Evermann reported in their *American Food and Game Fishes* that single hauls of commercial nets sometimes produced catches of 30,000 pounds or more, with the stripers averaging 70–80 pounds apiece. The nineteenth-century piscator Genio C. Scott reported that striped bass were once so tightly packed into the backwaters of the Seconnet River in Rhode Island that they had been frozen *en masse* with their dorsal fins projecting from the ice. The tremendous numbers of striped bass have since declined, partly as a result of decreased spawning success in polluted East Coast rivers.

The striped bass was known for many years by the generic name of *Roccus* (a Latinization of "rock"), a name coined by Dr. Samuel Mitchill in 1814. The striper is known as rock or rockfish because of its spawning activities in rocky rapids and its tendencies to feed along the rocky shores of bays and inlets. The species' noisy splashing and aggressiveness during spawning have consequently become known as "rock fights."

The striped bass became an ichthyological anomaly in the 1940s when fishery biologists in South Carolina noted that landlocked stripers in the newly constructed Santee-Cooper Reservoir were able to complete their entire life cycle in fresh water. This discovery prompted researchers to try to establish the striped bass as an landlocked game fish. Propagation was successful and stripers are now a game species in many reservoirs in the southern United States. The species must be maintained by stocking, however, because conditions for natural reproduction are rarely realized in inland reservoirs. Striped bass need large, deep rivers with a strong current to keep their eggs suspended and free of silt for the requisite 36–72 hours.

The striped bass is a popular trophy fish in inland waters and is caught on live bait, jigs, plugs, and spoons in the cool, deep water of reservoirs. Robert Barnwell Roosevelt offered some sound advice to nineteenth-century anglers on fishing for this squid hound:

> A rod made of a piece of bamboo, cut in two joints, will, until some awkward friend steps on and breaks it, answer as well as any other. . . . If you are a poor or careless man, buy a new flax line every year, and throw it away in the Fall, after being disgusted with it all the season. A well-made silk line is strong enough to hang oneself by, if the angler should be disgusted with life by his ill luck, and coated in this manner they will last a long time.

White Bass

Morone chrysops
Plate 106

Colloquial names: sand bass, striped bass, barfish, gray bass, silver bass, streaker, striped lake bass, black-striped bass

Scientific name:
Morone, of unknown origin
chrysops, Greek for "gold eye"

Distribution: Common in the central United States; absent from the eastern seaboard. Stocked into reservoirs throughout the continental United States. *Le silver bass du Canade* was also successfully propagated by Carbonnier in France during the 1870s.

Size: To 17 inches and a weight of 2 pounds, rarely larger. The typical hook-and-line specimen is about 1 pound. The world record was caught in the Colorado River of Texas in 1977 and weighed 5 lbs. 9 oz.

Status: Sport fish; not threatened in any state.

The white bass can be traced back to the annals of the naturalist Constantine Rafinesque, who angled his "golden-eyes perch" from the banks of the Ohio River in the early 1800s. The white bass is an abundant and widespread sport fish and is actively sought by anglers who catch it by the score during its feeding frenzies in lakes and its spring spawning runs into rivers and creeks. Minnows, small jigs, and spinners are the usual baits and under ideal conditions might return a dozen fish in a dozen casts.

The white bass grows rapidly, usually to 6 or more inches by the end of its first year. Three or four years is the average lifespan, although a specimen might occasionally live for six or seven years.

The white bass is an inhabitant of rivers and reservoirs, spending much of its time schooling in open waters over hard bottoms of sand, gravel, or rock. In rivers, the white bass avoids muddy or turbid flow and is most abundant in the deeper pools.

In reservoirs of the Great Plains, gizzard shad are the principal food of adult white bass, and as go the shad, so go the white bass. Accordingly, rapid growth of the white bass can be triggered by an "explosion" of the shad population. Hungry white bass will often pursue schools of gizzard shad, causing the shad to jump and "boil" the surface of the water in their frantic efforts to escape.

Wiper

Morone saxatilis × *Morone chrysops*

Plate 107

Colloquial names: Whiterock bass, rockfish hybrid, sunshine bass, silvers, *Morone* hybrid

Scientific name:
None. The name *wiper* is derived from the *w* in *white bass* and the *iper* in *striper.*

Distribution: Stocked into many reservoirs in the central United States, frequently escaping into rivers above and below impoundments.

Size: Commonly growing to 8–10 pounds. The world record is 23 lbs. 2 oz., caught in the Warrior River of Alabama in 1989.

Status: Artificial hybrid; not protected.

The wiper is a hybrid cross between the striped bass and the white bass. No naturally occurring hybrids between the two species of basses are known, and wipers are maintained through stocking and artificial propagation in hatcheries.

Wipers are believed to be incapable of reproduction, although some female wipers have been found to be full of eggs, and wipers have been caught among spawning white bass. The wiper is sometimes difficult to distinguish from the white and striped basses without relying on obscure characteristics. The overall body contour of the wiper is similar to that of the white bass, but the coloration and dark "striping" of the wiper is reminiscent of the striped bass. Wipers have two patches of teeth in the center of the tongue as does the striped bass; white bass usually have one. Still, some specimens are not identifiable morphologically so verification of a record fish may require that the species be determined in the laboratory by an electrophoretic protein analysis.

Wipers live five or six years and grow to 10 pounds or more. Like the white bass, they feed in open waters on gizzard shad, but wipers are also caught by anglers who "bottom fish" from shore with crayfish.

Yellow Bass

Morone mississippiensis

Plates 108–109

Colloquial names: gold bass, brassy bass, barfish, yellow perch, striped jack, streaker

Scientific name:
Morone, of unknown derivation
mississippiensis, so named for its occurrence in the Mississippi River

Distribution: Found principally in the Mississippi River and the lower Arkansas and Red River drainages. Occurring from southern Minnesota to Louisiana, southeast Oklahoma, and east Texas.

Size: Typically from 0.5 to 1 pound. The world record was caught in Lake Monroe, Indiana, in 1977, and weighed 2 lbs. 4 oz.

Status: Sport fish; of special concern in Minnesota.

The yellow or gold bass is closely allied to its silver congener, the white bass. For many years, the yellow bass was known scientifically as *Morone interrupta,* a name applied for the characteristic "fault line" that interrupts and offsets the lateral streaks on the fish's side.

The yellow bass is sometimes confused with the white bass, but the yellow bass has a slight connection between its dorsal fins and long, subequal second and third spines in the anal fin. The white bass is less becoming in profile than the yellow bass (at least to students of orthodontia) by reason of its exaggerated underbite. Male yellow bass frequently have a rich brassy luster about their sides in springtime, but the colors are less pronounced on the young and in fish from turbid water.

The habits and life history of the yellow bass closely parallel those of the white bass, and the two species are occasionally found together. Both species can be captured on hook-and-line by similar methods, but the yellow bass is generally taken in deeper water in lakes by trolling just off the bottom. The yellow bass is so prolific that it has become a stunted pest in some southern reservoirs, growing no larger than 6 inches.

In the southern states, barfish is the common appellation of the yellow bass. The name *barfish* is said to have originated in reference to the lateral stripes along the body, but it might have been more appropriately derived from the species' tendency to congregate upon shallow sandbars in the early morning hours.

White Perch

Morone americana

Plate 110

Colloquial names: silver perch, perch, gray perch

Scientific name:
Morone, of unknown derivation
americana, "American"

Distribution: An anadromous species along the East Coast. Transplanted into Lake Erie, Lake Ontario, and a few small lakes in Nebraska.

Size: Landlocked specimens grow to about 8 inches; seagoers generally reach 1 pound. The world record is 4 lbs. 12 oz. from Messalonskee Lake in Maine, caught in 1949. The Nebraska record is 1 lb. 6 oz.

Status: Introduced into our region; not protected in any state.

The white perch received its erroneous nickname of "perch" from Gmelin, who described the species in 1788 as *Perca americana,* or American perch. After the usual confusion associated with several other "original" descriptions of the species, the white perch was excised from the genus *Perca* (for it is not related to the perches) and placed into a new genus, *Morone,* as described by Dr. Samuel Latham Mitchill. Dr. Mitchill's *Morone* seems unfortunate in that it now stands as the valid name for four of our temperate basses, yet no one has been able to ascertain the literal translation or derivation of the name.

The white perch is similar in habits to our other temperate basses, although it is better adapted to landlocked reproduction than the striped bass. As a result, landlocked populations are normally self-sustaining, often to the point where they overpopulate and their growth is stunted. The only populations of white perch within the scope of our book are stocks that have been introduced into several Nebraska lakes. Because the species has a tendency to stunt in Nebraska, some of these populations have been systematically eradicated in recent years.

The white perch is native to the salt waters along the Atlantic Coast, where it ascends rivers in spring to spawn. The spawning runs of the white perch provide excellent panfishing, and the species is highly regarded as table fare. Jordan and Evermann ranked it among the tastiest of all fishes in their *American Food and Game Fishes,* saying "the only exception we feel disposed to make is the yellow perch."

Basses and Sunfishes

Family CENTRARCHIDAE

And the mighty sturgeon, Nahma,
Said to Ugudwash, the sun-fish,
To the bream, with scales of crimson,
"Take the bait of this great boaster,
Break the line of Hiawatha!"
Slowly upward, wavering, gleaming,
Rose the Ugudwash, the sun-fish,
Seized the line of Hiawatha,
Swung with all his weight upon it.
But when Hiawatha saw him
Slowly rising through the water,
Lifting up his disk refulgent,
Loud he shouted in derision,
"Esa! esa! shame upon you!
You are Ugudwash the sun-fish,
You are not the fish I wanted,
You are not the King of Fishes!"
—Henry Wadsworth Longfellow
  The Song of Hiawatha

The sunfishes are endemic treasures of North America and are probably better known to midwesterners than any other family of fishes. This widely distributed group consists of about 30 species of fishes in all sizes and colors, including the tiny, brilliantly hued orangespotted sunfish and the prodigious 20 pounds of the lunker largemouth bass. Many of the species have similar colors and ecological requirements, and their frequent crossbreeding sometimes makes identification difficult.

Sunfishes are known by a variety of common names. For instance, a bluegill might be called a bream (pronounced "brim") in the southern states, sunfish to the north, and sun-perch in between. Ichthyologists, however, have standardized the term *perch* for members of the *Percidae* or perch family,

including the yellow perch and walleye. A true sunfish can be recognized by the obvious connection between its spiny dorsal fin and soft dorsal fin, whereas in the true perches both fins are completely separated. The first European settlers in North America are probably to blame, for they undoubtedly christened the common sunfishes as *perch* because of the sunfishes' superficial resemblance to the common Old World perch.

In the Midwest, sunfishes can be found in almost any body of water, but they are most abundant in sluggish streams and warm ponds, lakes, and reservoirs. Sunfishes prefer the protective cover of rocks, tree stumps, weeds, and other vegetation and feed most actively under the diffuse lighting of early morning and evening.

Sunfishes feed primarily by sight, although they are somewhat nearsighted and even in crystal-clear water usually cannot see prey that is more than 6 feet away. The curiosity and appetite of the sunfishes are almost insatiable. Most of the smaller species can be lured by virtually any type of bait, but perhaps none is as satisfying and successful as the common earthworm fished beneath a bobbing float.

Sunfishes are somewhat gregarious in their nesting habits, and most follow a general spawning pattern. In spring or early summer, a male will use his tail to sweep a nest, usually a shallow, circular depression, into the soft mud or gravel bottom of quiet, shallow water. The males of the longear sunfish will aggregate into large breeding colonies and form a tightly packed, seemingly intolerable "Hooverville" of nests. In many species of sunfishes, the breeding

167

males become beautifully marked with distinctive, brilliant colors, a change that lures egg-laden females to the nest. The females will carry from 2000 to 25,000 eggs and oftentimes deposit them into more than one nest. The eggs are fertilized during their extrusion by the attending male, who then guards against predators until the eggs hatch and the fry disperse.

As Hiawatha so indignantly decried, the sunfish is "not the King of Fishes." Frequently, such smaller sunfishes as crappie or bluegill will overpopulate small ponds and lakes; and a pond full of 4-inch bluegills has no angling appeal save for the local raccoons. However, when the numbers of panfish are controlled by black bass or other predators, larger and healthier fish result. Despite their size, the smaller sunfishes are prized by young anglers and provide a fishery throughout the Great Plains, often in ponds and intermittent streams where few other species can exist.

Largemouth Bass

Micropterus salmoides

Plates 111–112

Colloquial names: bigmouth bass, moss-back, straw bass, green trout, slough bass, Oswego bass, mud bass, chub, jumper, speckled hen, cow bass, river bass, lake bass

Scientific name:
Micropterus, Greek for "small fin"
salmoides, Latin for "troutlike"

Distribution: Native to most of the eastern half of the United States. Now stocked in all of the continental states.

Size: Frequently grows to 6 pounds in the north central Great Plains. In the southern states, the Florida subspecies commonly exceeds 10 pounds. The world record is 22 lbs. 4 oz., set in Georgia in 1932.

Status: Sport fish, not protected.

The largemouth's unmatched versatility, showmanship, and cunning make it one of the most sought after game fishes in the world. The original distribution of this species included much of eastern North America, but successful introductions during the past 100 years have made it possible for anglers throughout Europe, South America, and Africa to share in the tradition of bass fishing.

The largemouth bass had a rather inauspicious and confusing beginning in ichthyology. In the late 1700s, skins of the largemouth were shipped overseas to Linnaeus by colonists in hopes that he would name the species. He never did. But in 1802, the French naturalist Lacépède published the original account of the species, *Labrus salmoides,* on the basis of a drawing and simple description that he had received from Carolina. The drawing was so poorly executed and the description so incomplete that later researchers could not decide with certainty whether the fish had been a smallmouth or largemouth bass. In 1881, after many other descriptions had appeared under various scientific names, the problem of the appropriate name for the largemouth was resolved by Dr. James A. Henshall in his *Book of the Black Bass.* Henshall suggested that because of the words *large-mouthed* and *common* in Lacépède's description, and because of the extremely limited distribution of the smallmouth bass in "Carolina," Lacépède's bass *had* to be a largemouth. Because the largemouth bass no longer was considered a true *Labrus* (the type genus of Old World wrasses described by Linnaeus in 1758), the species had already been excised from that genus and family. The genus *Micropterus,* which Lacépède applied in 1802 to the smallmouth bass, is the oldest generic name directly applicable to the black basses. The original trivial name of *salmoides* was conserved by Henshall because it was the very first epithet ascribed to the largemouth. The name of the largemouth bass now stands as Henshall contended it should, *Micropterus salmoides.* Interestingly, the nomenclature had been so confused prior to Henshall's proposal that the smallmouth bass was known as *Micropterus salmoides* for many years.

All of the centrarchid basses (or "black basses") depend on their eyesight to help them locate prey. The largemouth, however, seems better suited to murky waters than any of its *Micropterus* kin and is usually most abundant in the warm, still waters of lakes, bayous, and stream pools. Although prey fishes seem best able to see and avoid a hungry largemouth during daylight, the largemouth has an inherent advantage during the dimmer hours of dawn and dusk, when it can still see relatively well and is less conspicuous to the prey. Adult largemouths feed on fish, crayfish, frogs, and other unsuspecting animals that might happen within striking distance. Although it can be enticed to strike a variety of baits and lures, the largemouth's unpredictable behavior and appetite make it a difficult sport fish to master.

Male largemouths form their nests in the spring, usually as simple, shallow depressions that are "tailswept" into soft silt or mud. Active nests might also be used by minnows or suckers whose young will benefit from the largemouth's protective instincts. The largemouth has some cannibalistic tendencies, however, so the strategy of the uninvited "nesters" is not without some risk.

Two subspecies make up the largemouth bass: the northern largemouth and the Florida largemouth. The subspecies are nearly identical in appearance (our illustrations represent the natural range of colors in the species), but the Florida strain tends to have more lateral line scales (70 or more as compared to 68 or less in the northern) and a broken lateral band. However, the two subspecies freely hybridize, and experts suggest there is no foolproof method of identification. The faster-growing Florida subspecies requires perennially warm water and is native to the extreme southeast, but recent stocks have made it available in most of the warmer southern states, including Texas and California.

On the second of June, 1932, 18-year-old George Washington Perry set the standard by which all largemouth bass have been measured. Perry was fishing from a homemade wooden boat in a slough called Montgomery Lake on the Ocmulgee River in rural Georgia. With his $1.33 baitcasting rig and his only lure, a wooden Creek Chub Wigglefish, Perry hooked and landed a world record 22 lbs. 4 oz. largemouth bass. Perry, who was fishing to put food on the table, cleaned and ate the fish after having its weight and measurements certified. For the past half-century, anglers have been targeting Perry's record. If the record is broken, the fish might come from the "San Diego Lakes," a series of Southern California reservoirs that have been stocked with Florida largemouth and have consistently produced 18-pound fish. The next world-record largemouth is being tabbed as a "million dollar fish," the impending result of what will surely be scores of endorsement offers from tackle and boat manufacturers and other companies associated with the sport of fishing.

Smallmouth Bass

Micropterus dolomieui

Plates 113, 115–116

Colloquial names: black bass, brownie, bronzeback, smallie, redeye, jumper, trout bass, white trout, brown trout, gold bass, green bass, swago bass, streaked-cheek river bass

Scientific name:

Micropterus, Greek for "small fin" *dolomieui*, after the French mineralogist Dolomieu, a friend of Lacépède, the species' authority

Distribution: Found over much of the eastern half of the United States in clear rivers and reservoirs. Becoming less common west of the Mississippi and absent from the Great Plains and western United States except where stocked.

Size: Commonly attaining a weight of 3–4 pounds and a length of 20 inches. The world record of 11 lbs. 15 oz. was caught in July 1955 at Dale Hollow Lake in Kentucky.

Status: Of special concern in Mississippi.

The black bass is eminently an American fish; he has the faculty of asserting himself and making himself completely at home wherever placed. He is plucky, game, brave and unyielding to the last when hooked. He has the arrowy rush of the trout, the untiring strength and bold leap of the salmon, while he has a system of fighting tactics peculiarly his own. I consider him, inch for inch and pound for pound, the gamest fish that swims.
—James A. Henshall
  Book of the Black Bass, 1881

The sporting qualities of the smallmouth bass and the aesthetic beauty of its habitat afford the species an immense popularity among anglers. The smallmouth's native range included most of east-central North America, but stocking programs have established populations throughout much of the western United States and on other continents.

The smallmouth bass is a fish of many colors, being in its various habitats and stages of life black, brown, golden, green, or bronze as its many vernaculars will attest. Because of its exceptional variability, the smallmouth has been described as a new species no fewer than 14 times, with all of these "new species" eventually referable to the original type as described by the French naturalist Lacépède in 1802. Constantine Rafinesque, who caught most of his specimens on hook-and-line from the Ohio River, was the worst offender, having described six different "species" only on the basis of size and color variation. Lacépède described the smallmouth bass from a preserved fish that he received from the United States. The specimen, however had a peculiar anomaly: The last few rays of the soft dorsal fin had been separated from the rest of the fin as if from some bite or other injury. Lacépède, thinking the fish had three dorsal fins, proceeded to name the genus *Micropterus*, Greek for "small fin." *Micropterus* thus stands as the prioritized genus of our black basses.

The smallmouth has been divided into two subspecies, the Neosho and the northern. The Neosho smallmouth was originally found throughout southern Ozark streams but is now restricted to a few streams in Arkansas and some headwater drainages of the Neosho-Grand River in Oklahoma. The northern smallmouth is native to the upper Mississippi River drainage, but it was widely stocked by the railroads into the Ozarks and has consequently hybridized with much of the original Neosho population.

Smallmouth bass are at home in lakes and in small rivers with clear, unpolluted, permanently flowing waters. In streams they commonly occur over gravelly bottoms near the cover of large rocks or tangled roots, oftentimes where the current is barely perceptible. In lakes and reservoirs smallmouths frequent moderately deep water and are usually found along undercut banks and rocky ledges.

Adult smallmouths feed mostly on crayfish and fish. In spring and fall, anglers seek smallmouths in habitats varying from stagnant, weed-choked shallows to deep open water. Contrary to an old myth, water temperature is not always the most important factor controlling the distribution of smallmouths in a lake, and in the absence of competition from largemouth bass, smallmouths are often found in habitats typical of that species.

Spotted Bass

Micropterus punctulatus

Plate 114

Colloquial names: Kentucky bass, line-sides, diamond bass

Scientific name:
Micropterus, Greek for "small fin"
punctulatus, Latin for "dotted"

Distribution: Includes the southern Great Plains from the Kansas Flint Hills through eastern Texas; sporadic eastward to the forested streams of the Appalachians. Stocked into reservoirs in many southern and western states.

Size: Growing to 3 pounds in streams, larger in reservoirs. The record spotted bass of 8 lbs. 15 oz. was caught from Lewis Smith Lake in Alabama in 1978.

Status: Of special concern in North Carolina.

Once widely believed to be a hybrid between the smallmouth and largemouth basses, the spotted or Kentucky bass is a relative newcomer to American fisheries. The species was first described in 1819 by the French naturalist Rafinesque, who named it *Calliurus punctulatus: Calliurus* meaning "beautiful tail," a reference to the colorful tail of his immature specimen. Later researchers assumed Rafinesque's specimen was a smallmouth bass and placed it into synonymy with the smallmouth. Not until 1927 was the species recognized by ichthyologists as distinct, when Dr. Carl Hubbs named it *Micropterus pseudaplites.* Later, upon the recognition that Hubbs's species was the same as that described by Rafinesque, the epithet *punctula-tus* was resurrected and *Micropterus punctulatus* became the valid name.

Although its genetic affinities lie with the smallmouth bass, the spotted bass is easily confused with the largemouth. A spotted bass can be distinguished by its orange or scarlet-red iris, broadly connected dorsal fins, chalk-white belly, smaller mouth, and the prominent rows of spots on the upper belly.

The spotted bass is well adapted to the deeper waters of southern reservoirs but is also the most abundant bass in the main channels of many streams. Spotted bass are most successful in waters that are somewhat warmer and siltier than those that support native populations of smallmouths and will sometimes outcompete or "replace" smallmouths in degraded streams. The eggs of the spotted bass also have a short incubation period, which leaves the species less susceptible to predation or other natural calamities. The spawning regimens of the spotted and smallmouth basses are similar, and the two species will occasionally hybridize.

Its highly touted reputation as a game fish and its ability to survive adverse water conditions have made the spotted bass an increasingly popular component of sport fisheries. Known to many anglers as Kentucky bass, the "spot" is a tribute to the work of Dr. Hubbs, whose studies helped the species gain notoriety as a sport fish in Kentucky. Adult spotted bass subsist principally on a diet of insects, crayfish, and fish and can be caught by the same methods that take other basses. We suggest the following method for enterprising youngsters on a slow, hot day:

A boy having caught a sun-fish, runs his hook through its nose and out at its mouth, covering the point with a lively worm. Other sun-fish, seeing their fellow have all to himself a fine, fat worm which he seems unable to master, collect round him, and by their numbers attract the bass, who dashes in among them, and while the rest make off, swallows the one with the worm, and of course himself falls a prey to the ingenious young fisherman (*Brown's Angler's Almanac*).

Guadalupe Bass

Micropterus treculi

Plate 117

Colloquial names: Texas spotted bass

Scientific name:
Micropterus, Greek for "small fin"
treculi, after its discoverer

Distribution: Streams and reservoirs of south-central Texas, native to the Colorado, Guadalupe, and San Antonio river drainages.

Size: Generally about 12 inches and 1 pound, to a maximum of about 2 pounds in its native streams. The hook-and-line record was caught in Lake Travis, Texas, in 1983 and weighed 3 lbs. 11 oz.

Status: Of special concern in its native Texas habitat.

The guadalupe bass is native to the sparkling clear, rocky-bottomed streams of the Edwards Plateau in central Texas. Although the species has been established within a few reservoirs and streams outside of its native habitat, the range of the guadalupe bass still occurs entirely within Texas.

The guadalupe bass is most closely related to—and for many years was considered to be a subspecies of—the spotted bass, hence the old common name of Texas spotted bass. The markings and color pattern of the guadalupe, however, frequently approach those of the smallmouth bass, and the guadalupe is sometimes confused with that species. The guadalupe can be separated from the smallmouth on the basis of its fewer lateral line scales (averaging 65 in the guadalupe and usually more than 70 in the smallmouth) and the different number of rays in the soft dorsal fin (usually 12 in the guadalupe and 13 or 14 in the smallmouth). Because the smallmouth bass was not native to central Texas, its introduction and subsequent hybridization with the guadalupe bass have threatened the native "pure strain" guadalupe. Pure guadalupes are still common in the headwaters of the San Antonio and Llano rivers in central Texas, but are becoming increasingly difficult to find along the lower reaches of these streams.

The guadalupe has a stronger preference for flowing waters than other black basses, and stocking programs in reservoirs have met with limited success. The species is most at home in fast currents along the lower ends of riffles and runs, where it feeds on crustaceans, minnows, and larval insects that wash downstream.

Northern Rock Bass

Ambloplites rupestris

Plate 118

Colloquial names: goggle-eye, rock bass, redeye, garguncle

Scientific names:
Ambloplites, Greek for "blunt armature"
rupestris, Latin for "living among the rocks"

Distribution: Great Lakes and much of the northeastern United States; absent from the coast. In our range, common in Minnesota and eastern Iowa, Neosho-Grand drainage in Oklahoma, and the Osage, Gasconade, and Meramec rivers in central Missouri. Transplanted but uncommon in most other Great Plains states.

Size: Growing to a maximum of about 10 inches in length. The world record on hook-and-line weighed 3 pounds.

Status: Sport fish; not threatened in any state.

Three species of rock basses occur in the central United States. All have similar habits and habitat requirements and sport the brilliant scarlet-red iris and the five or six anal spines that are so characteristic of the genus. The northern rock bass, which is the most widespread of the three and has been widely introduced throughout the Great Plains, is characteristically found in the clearer streams of the eastern United States and is common in a few lakes in the more northern portion of its range. This species can be distinguished from the other *Ambloplites* by its darker, bolder spotting and by the black border that develops on the edge of the anal and pelvic fins in breeding males.

The northern rock bass is typically found around tangled roots, rocky ledges, or trees that are submerged in slow-moving runs or pools. Goggle-eyes might forage at any time of the day but are most active at dawn and dusk when they are easily caught by anglers using small spinners for lures. Minnows, crayfish, and madtoms that are "bumped" along the bottom of pools make excellent baits during daylight hours.

Shadow Bass

Ambloplites ariommus

Plate 119

Colloquial names: southern rock bass, goggle-eye, redeye, rock bass

Scientific name:
Ambloplites, Greek for "blunt armature"
ariommus, Greek for "large-eyed"

Distribution: Southeastern United States, especially near the Gulf Coast from Louisiana to the Florida panhandle. In our region, common in the Ouachita drainage of southeast Arkansas and in the Current and Black river systems of southeast Missouri and northeast Arkansas.

Size: Smallest of the *Ambloplites*, growing to a maximum of 7–8 inches.

Status: Common throughout its range.

The shadow bass was originally recognized as being distinct from the northern rock bass in the 1930s and was widely regarded as the southern rock bass subspecies for many years. The shadow bass is similar in habitats and requirements to the northern rock bass, but it is deeper bodied, has the sides boldly blotched, and typically does not grow as large.

Both the shadow bass and the Ozark rock bass are the true southern species of rock basses. The shadow bass, however, will hybridize extensively with the northern rock bass, and widespread transplants of the two species have consequently made some identifications difficult. Semblances of both species or their hybrids are thought to occur in northeast Oklahoma and in the southeast Missouri Ozarks.

Like all *Ambloplites*, shadow basses occur in loose aggregations that stratify in and about the cover of rocky banks or submerged trees and are most frequently associated with smallmouth bass, bluegills, and green sunfish. The shadow bass is carnivorous and feeds principally on crayfish, minnows, and larval insects.

Ozark Rock Bass

Ambloplites constellatus

Plate 120

Colloquial names: goggle-eye, rock bass, redeye

Scientific name:
Ambloplites, Greek for "blunt armature" *constellatus,* Latin for "with stars," a reference to the species' clustered pattern of spots

Distribution: Mostly restricted to the White River drainage of southern Missouri and northern Arkansas.

Size: Up to 10 inches, the average hook-and-line catch being 6–7 inches.

Status: Common throughout its range.

The Ozark rock bass is largely restricted to the White River drainage of Arkansas and southwestern Missouri and was only recently (1977) described as a species different from the northern rock bass. The Ozark rock bass differs principally in its lighter overall color and in its irregular and interrupted pattern of spots on its back and lower sides. Like other species of *Ambloplites,* young Ozark rock basses have a brassy sheen and faint dusky blotching on the face and sides. This species has been transplanted into other drainages in Missouri and Arkansas, but it is not well established and is not known to hybridize with our other rock basses.

Because the Ozark rock bass is not widespread and was so recently differentiated from the northern rock bass, little is known of its habits. But like the other *Ambloplites,* the Ozark rock bass occurs in clear-water streams and favors pools or slow-moving runs from 2 to 5 feet deep. The species is one of the most abundant panfishes in the Buffalo River of Arkansas and also occurs in and about Lake Taneycomo, Table Rock Reservoir, and Bull Shoals Reservoir in southern Missouri and Arkansas.

Warmouth

Chaenobryttus gulosus

Plates 121–123

Colloquial names: warmouth bass, goggle-eye, stumpknocker, wood bass, mud bass, bigmouth, black warmouth, perchmouth bream, yawnmouth perch, jugmouth, mud chub, Indian fish

Scientific name:
Chaenobryttus, from the Greek *chaeno* meaning "to yawn" and the Greek *bryttus,* an old synonym for *Lepomis,* probably a reference to the teeth on the palatine
gulosus, Latin for "large-mouthed"

Distribution: Abundant in the lowlands of the southeastern United States; occurring sporadically as far west as New Mexico. Occasional in the northern states as far north as Lake Erie and southeastern Minnesota. Mostly absent from the Great Plains.

Size: About 10 inches and 0.5 pounds. The world record is 2 lbs. 7 oz., caught in the Yellow River in Florida in 1985.

Status: Not threatened in any state.

This small, sedentary sunfish befits well its scientific designation of *gulosus,* or "large-mouthed." The name *warmouth* is probably derived from the common name of Indian fish and the striking "Indian warpaint" pattern of facial bars that radiate from the fish's red eye. The warmouth is the only species within the monotypic *Chaenobryttus,* although the closely related green sunfish was formerly included in the same genus.

The warmouth is a solitary or loosely gregarious panfish that is most at home over the muddy, weedy bottoms of swamps, sluggish ditches, and "river lakes" (oxbows). This timid fish spends most of its time skulking within the dimly lit hollows of weedbeds, brushpiles, and tree stumps, occasionally darting out to make a meal of an unwary crayfish or stray minnow.

Within the central United States, the warmouth occurs naturally in the lowlands of southeastern Kansas, southern Iowa, and all of our southern states. Its absence from the western Plains is attributable to the lack of backwaters, flooded lowlands, and similar habitats. Warmouths exhibit a wider range of body colors than most sunfishes and can be difficult to recognize. Individuals from swamps might be mottled a dark purplish-brown and at first glance appear to be wholly different from the sandy-brown specimens of upland reservoirs.

The warmouth has a relatively low reproductive potential and is sometimes used to establish panfisheries in ponds and reservoirs. Although it rarely exceeds a weight of 0.5 pounds, the warmouth is actively pursued as sport in the southern states by fly fishermen. In the deep south, the "swamp" warmouth is renowned for its stubborn resistance when hooked, yet it rarely receives any invitations to dinner, its strong-tasting flesh being most aptly likened to its southern vernacular—mud bass!

Green Sunfish

Lepomis cyanellus

Plates 124, 127

Colloquial names: sunperch, black perch, bluespotted sunfish, green perch, goggle-eye, branch perch, perch, rock bass, pond perch, shade perch, rubbertail, ricefield slick, redeye, sand bass, blue bass, blue and green sunfish, buffalo sunfish

Scientific name:
Lepomis, Greek for "scaled operculum," all species of this genus having scaled cheeks and gill covers
cyanellus, Greek for "blue"

Distribution: Found throughout the middle United States, including the Great Lakes. West from Alabama to New Mexico and Colorado.

Size: Up to 9 inches in length, but usually much smaller. The world record is 2 lbs. 2 oz.

Status: Sport fish; not threatened in any state.

"Ubiquitous" is perhaps the best way to characterize the abundant green sunfish. Although this species is absent from the western reaches of the Dakotas, it occurs in virtually every natural body of water in the central United States. As a result, the green sunfish is known by a plethora of colloquial names, including such misnomers as rock bass and perch.

The green sunfish is a prolific colonizer and is tolerant of warm, turbid water, making it the most abundant and adaptable of all the sunfishes. It is typically one of the last species of sunfishes to disappear from streams during drought and is usually among the first to repopulate. In most ponds and reservoirs, green sunfish do so well at "populating" that they frequently outstrip food supplies, resulting in an impoundment teeming with stunted 3- and 4-inch fish.

The green sunfish is most abundant in the quiet pools of creeks and rivers and along lake shorelines, where it feeds within the protective continuity of rock ledges, weed beds, and boat docks. The species' large mouth and voracious appetite are "bad medicine" for insects and fishes up to three-fourths its own length! Consequently, in smaller prairie streams, the green sunfish (and occasionally the largemouth bass) will sometimes occur in small pools to the virtual exclusion of other species of fish. The aggressive gluttony of the green sunfish is probably best manifest, however, in its legendary bait-stealing propensity; most anglers who have fished worms in hopes of catching pan-sized fish have probably coined a few names of their own for this pesky little thief!

Bluegill

Lepomis macrochirus

Plates 125, 128

Colloquial names: bream, coppernose bream, blue sunfish, blue perch, sunperch, copperhead, dollardee, pond perch, gold perch, chainside, sunfish, blue joe, baldface

Scientific name:
Lepomis, Greek for "scaled operculum" *macrochirus,* Greek for "large hand," probably a reference to the general outline of the body

Distribution: Native to the eastern United States, except for the far northeast. Becoming uncommon in streams of the High Plains. Now successfully stocked into all 48 continental states.

Size: Commonly growing to 9 inches and 0.75 pounds, but populations sometimes stunt at 6 inches or less. The largest bluegill ever taken on hook-and-line weighed 4 lbs. 12 oz., was 15 inches long, and had a girth of 18.25 inches.

Status: Not threatened in any state.

The black "earflap," small mouth, and powder-blue throat are the universal characteristics of the bluegill. Its stocky body, powerful endurance, and insatiable appetite are also widely known, combining to make it the gamest and most popular of all the sunfishes.

Bluegills travel in schools, usually near shore in water from 1 to 20 feet deep. The bigger bluegills occupy the deepest water and spend their time in loosely knit groups of 20 or 30 fish. The bluegill's diet is comprised of zooplankton, microcrustaceans, snails, insects, and fish. Its taste for fishes is governed by the size of its mouth—too small to partake of any species excepting the smaller minnows.

The bluegill is the mainstay of the fishery in many small ponds and lakes and is also common in our clearer creeks and rivers. Bluegills have a seemingly uncontrollable urge to bite at worms and crickets on a hook, and once a school of 'gills is located, the angler might well catch every member of the group. The bluegill does not take bait with a heady, uncalculated rush as do the basses but quietly inhales its prey, beginning to struggle for liberty upon the discovery that it is no longer free. The bluegill is a valiant fighter when hooked and is extraordinarily strong for its size. Adult bluegills grow as much in girth as they do in length, and specimens 1 pound or larger resemble—in size and outline—the dinner plate where they frequently end up.

Bluegills breed in spring and summer in 1 or 2 feet of water. Some old-time fishermen insist that bluegills predict the summer's weather based on the water depth chosen for their nesting grounds. By nesting in shallow water, bluegills are supposedly predicting a rise in the water level. Conversely, nests in deeper waters are a portent of drought, because the bluegills are "expecting" the water level to drop. We pass that on for those of you still skeptical of the national forecasting service!

Redbreast Sunfish

Lepomis auritus

Plates 126, 129

Colloquial names: yellowbelly sunfish, longear bream, red brim, sunperch, red-bellied bream, redheaded bream, robin, red perch, tobacco box, flatfish, leather ear, blackeared pondfish

Scientific name:
Lepomis, Greek for "scaled operculum"
auritus, Latin for "eared"

Distribution: Common in Atlantic Coast states east of the Alleghenies, from Maine to Alabama and Florida. Introduced into Texas.

Size: Commonly reaching 8–10 inches in length; occasionally attaining 1 pound. The world record weighed 2 lbs. 1 oz. and was caught in the Suwannee River of Florida in 1988.

Status: Not threatened in any state.

The redbreast has the distinction of being the first member of the sunfish family to receive a scientific name. The species was described in 1758 by Linnaeus, who had received a specimen from the vicinity of Philadelphia. Linnaeus christened the species as *auritus,* meaning "eared," in consideration of the greatly elongated and flexible opercular flap. Male redbreasts have longer and broader earflaps than females and are more brightly colored during the breeding season, when their bellies develop hues of bright yellow-orange or red.

The redbreast sunfish is not native to the central United States but occurs within our range in the eastern two-thirds of Texas, where it was established in rivers and reservoirs by widespread stocking. The redbreast is most abundant in the clear waters of the central Texas hill country, where it is known appropriately as yellowbelly, occurring in the company of the native bluegill, green sunfish, and spotted sunfish. The species is also occasionally taken along the Texas border in Oklahoma, Arkansas, and Louisiana.

The redbreast is one of the most common sunfishes of the southeastern United States, where it is billed as a strong fighter and a favorite food fish. The species frequently attains weights of 0.75 to 1 pound, putting the redbreast among the elite company of the bluegill and redear as the "kings of sunfishes."

Redear Sunfish

Lepomis microlophus

Plates 130, 133

Colloquial names: shellcracker, yellow bream, Georgia bream, cherry gill, Texas improved bream, stumpknocker, branch perch, strawberry bass, pond perch

Scientific name:
Lepomis, Greek for "scaled operculum"
microlophus, Greek for "small nape"

Distribution: Native to all the Gulf Coast states and presently stocked into ponds and reservoirs in most Midwest states.

Size: A large sunfish, averaging 8–10 inches and a weight of 0.5 pounds. The world record weighed 4 lbs. 13 oz. and was caught from Merritt's Mill Pond in Florida in 1986.

Status: Sport fish; not threatened in any state.

The redear is a large sunfish with an affinity for warm, sluggish southern waters. Although mostly a fish of the Gulf coastal plain, the redear is now stocked throughout most of the central United States. Its large size (up to 12 inches) and rapid growth rate make the redear a popular stocker for farm ponds and county lakes.

Adult redears are most easily recognized by their small mouths, long, attenuated pectoral fins, and the reddish border of their "ear" flaps. The male redear is more brightly colored than the female and sports an ear border of bright cherry red. The edge of the flap in females and young is usually a pale orange. The pumpkinseed is the only similar sunfish with a bright red "earring," but the redear lacks the iridescent blue-green facial bars of that species.

The redear is most at home in clear water that has an abundant growth of submerged vegetation. Adult redears prefer 5–10 feet of water and typically live near the bottom of lakes and ponds, where they feed on snails and insect larvae. The redear uses its flattened "throat teeth" to crush the shells of snails and freshwater clams, habits that have earned it the nickname of shellcracker.

The redear is a dandy panfish, although its bottom-dwelling habits require modified "sunfishing" techniques. Late spring and early summer, when male redears are aggressively guarding their nests, produce the best catches. Worms fished on or near the bottom in 5–10 feet of water will usually produce a catch, but a redear is apt to drop the bait if it feels any resistance from the fishing gear.

Pumpkinseed

Lepomis gibbosus

Plates 131, 134

Colloquial names: common sunfish, sunny, common perch, kivvy, yellow belly, round sunfish, flatfish, tobacco box, crapet jaune, quiver, roach, sun bass

Scientific name:
Lepomis, Greek for "scaled operculum" *gibbosus,* Latin for "formed like the full moon," a reference to the outline of the body

Distribution: Principally a species of the northeastern United States and Quebec and Ontario. Coming into our range in the eastern edge of the Dakotas, north-central Nebraska, Minnesota, and Iowa.

Size: Usually 6–8 inches, but exceptional specimens might reach 9 inches and 0.75 pounds. The world record is 1 lb. 6 oz., caught in Oswego Pond, New York, in 1985.

Status: Of special concern in Missouri.

The nickname of "sunfish" probably originated with the common sunny or pumpkinseed because of its bright lemon-yellow belly, and habit of shimmering and mirroring the light of the sun with its every change of direction. "It is a very beautiful and compact fish," wrote Henry David Thoreau in *A Week on the Concord and Merrimack Rivers,* "perfect in all its parts, looking like a brilliant coin fresh from the mint."

The pumpkinseed is a delightful cooperator of young and inexperienced anglers—a string, a hook, and an angleworm being sufficient to lure its strike. George Brown Goode paid such tribute to this small, but gamy panfish in his *American Fishes:*

The "Pumpkin seed" and the perch are the first trophies of the boy angler. Many are the memories of truant days dreamed away by pond or brook side, with twine, pole and pin-hook, and of the slow homeward trudge, doubtful what his reception will be at home; pole gone, line broken, hooks lost, the only remnant of the morning's glory a score of lean, sun-dried perches and Sunnies, and mayhap, a few eels and bullheads, ignominiously strung through the gills upon a willow withe, and trailing, sometimes dropping from weary hands, in the roadside dust.

The vernacular *pumpkinseed* is not derived, as one might suspect, from the orange and ochre spots that dot the fish's sides but rather from the gibbous outline of the species' body, which is reminiscent of the contoured seeds of the pumpkin.

The male pumpkinseed becomes pugnacious during the breeding season, seeking to clear his nesting ground of any intruders, especially his "brother" males. The male endeavors to establish his territory by chasing and brutishly biting at the fins of any intruding rivals, a battle so intensely fought that the water is sometimes clouded by the sand, silt, and vegetation torn from the bed of the stream. Nests are sometimes grouped tightly together within a breeding ground, but each nest is usually surrounded by modest curtains of aquatic vegetation. The spawning habits of the pumpkinseed are similar to those of other sunfishes, having been loosely described as "promiscuous polygamy." Pumpkinseeds hybridize freely with most other sunfishes, and several of these crosses were errantly described in early literature as distinct species of sunfishes.

Orangespotted Sunfish

Lepomis humilis

Plates 132, 135

Colloquial names: orangespot, pumpkinseed, redspotted sunfish, dwarf sunfish, pygmy sunfish

Scientific name:
Lepomis, Greek for "scaled operculum"
humilis, Latin for "humble"

Distribution: Occurring from eastern North Dakota and southern Minnesota south through eastern Texas and Louisiana. Also common in the Ohio Valley and the central High Plains.

Size: Typically about 3 inches long, occasionally to 4 or 5 inches.

Status: Not protected in any state.

The tiny orangespotted sunfish is one of our prettiest native fishes. On first glance, the spawning male seems an artistic invention, his body washed in dazzling iridescence of sapphire blues and emerald greens, and his belly and brightly colored fins dipped in pigments of vivid red-orange. A net full of the same from the dingy waters of a muddy creek is a spectacular sight. But nature, in dimorphic irony, has bedecked the female orangespot with a drab olive-brown, an unseemly complement to her garishly colored mate.

Although they are occasionally found in ponds and reservoirs, orangespots are most common in the sandy or silty pools of creeks and small rivers, where they tolerate low flow, high water temperatures, and siltation better than most sunfishes. Indeed, the orangespot's adaptability seems to have been inbred expressly for the harsh life of the Great Plains. Consequently, orangespots occur throughout the central and southern Plains, much in the pattern of the green sunfish, with which it is usually found.

The orangespot feeds principally on young crayfish and immature aquatic insects, but its voracious appetite and moderate-sized mouth prompt it to steal fishing worms with frustrating regularity. Although orangespotted sunfish are too small to be of much value as sport fish, a 3-inch male in full breeding colors might well evoke as much admiration as any 5-pound bass.

Spotted Sunfish

Lepomis punctatus

Plates 136, 138

Colloquial names: red perch, chinquapin perch, spotted bream, scarlet sunfish, stumpknocker

Scientific name:
Lepomis, Greek for "scaled operculum"
punctatus, Latin for "spotted"

Distribution: Mostly the southeastern United States. Into our range in southeast Missouri, Arkansas, southeastern Oklahoma, and eastern Texas.

Size: Generally less than 6 inches in length, but occasionally growing to 9 inches and a weight of 0.5 pounds.

Status: Of special concern in Kentucky.

The spotted sunfish is an obscure but splendidly colored panfish. The spawning males are brilliantly marked with scarlet and magenta spots on the belly and lower sides, with iridescent hues of crimson and blue in the upper back. The female is less garishly colored with spots of inconspicuous orange or muted yellow. Spotted sunfish can also be recognized by three indistinct stripes on the upper part of the gill cover. Varieties of the spotted sunfish from Florida, Georgia, and other states in the deep South are marked with brown, blue, or black spots instead of orange or red and were formerly considered to be different species. Immature spotted sunfish are sometimes "unspotted" and bear a superficial resemblance to the tiny bantam sunfish, with which they sometimes occur.

The spotted sunfish shares with the warmouth the curious nickname of stumpknocker, purportedly derived from the fish's peculiar habit of leaping unabatedly into stumps and branches in attempts to dislodge insects for food. The species subsists principally on insects, small crayfish, and other crustaceans. We have caught spotted sunfish on occasion in streams by the use of worms, minnows, small spinners, and poppers but have never coaxed more than two individuals from any one pool. Spotted sunfish are fond of clear, heavily vegetated streams and lakes. The species is common in many southern reservoirs, in the clear streams and ditches of southeastern Texas, and among the backwaters of some Ozark streams.

Longear Sunfish

Lepomis megalotis

Plates 137, 139

Colloquial names: cherry bream, long-eared bream, big-eared sunfish, pumpkinseed, creek perch, blackears, bloody sunfish, redeyed sunfish, brilliant sunfish, tobacco box

Scientific name:
Lepomis, Greek for "scaled operculum"
megalotis, Greek for "great ear"

Distribution: Occurring across the central United States from Michigan and Pennsylvania to the Gulf Coast and northeastern Mexico. Absent from the northern and western Great Plains.

Size: Males are larger than females and reach a maximum size of about 7 inches. The world record is 1 lb. 12 oz. from Elephant Butte Lake in New Mexico, caught in 1985.

Status: Protected or of special concern in Iowa, Wisconsin, and New York.

The longear is among the most beautiful of our native fishes. The male is more brilliantly colored than the female, and during the spawning period he sports a handsome breast of deep vermilion and rusty sides with mottlings of emerald green or blue. Because the species varies geographically, one cannot expect a Kansas fish to look the same as a specimen from a Louisiana bayou, any more than we might expect a Nebraskan to speak with a Texas accent. The longear is sometimes referred to as tobacco box, because its long, earlike opercular flap is sometimes rounded like the lid of a tobacco tin.

The longear is most abundant in our region from southern Missouri and southeastern Kansas through Texas, where it is the characteristic sunfish of clean, gravel-bottomed creeks and small rivers. Longears are most common in and about shallow pools or slow runs with a scarcely perceptible flow. In the pristine rivers of the Missouri Ozarks, male longears build nests in colonies during early summer, when their curious habits and effusive displays can be observed by any attentive canoeist. A breeding male longear will often crowd his nest to within a few inches of his neighbor's and subsequently defend his nestlings against all predators, including occasional visits from the cannibalistic fish-next-door!

Because the longear rarely exceeds 6 inches in length, it is not usually sought by anglers. Many, however, will affirm the longear's unabashed eagerness to take most any offering. In fact, inexperienced anglers might be well advised to hide their worms behind a tackle box, log, or other set object to conceal them from ravenous longears!

Dollar Sunfish

Lepomis marginatus

Plate 140

Colloquial names: Florida long-eared sunfish, red-eyed perch

Scientific name:
Lepomis, Greek for "scaled operculum" *marginatus*, Latin for "margined," probably named for the opercular lobe, which sometimes has a pale green margin

Distribution: Restricted to the lowlands in the southeastern United States, as far north as southern Arkansas and southeast Oklahoma.

Size: A maximum length of 6 inches.

Status: Of special concern in Kentucky.

The dollar sunfish is a rather obscure species, so named for its small size and compact rounded outline, which is said to resemble a silver dollar. The species was originally described in 1855, but later researchers considered the fish a subspecies of the longear sunfish. Dollar sunfish have shorter earflaps than the longear, and the length of the flap is usually equal to its width. In the deep south, the dollar sunfish typically has four scale rows on the cheek, compared to six in the longear, and has 12 rays in the pectoral fins, as opposed to 14 or 15 in the latter. Our specimens from East Texas have fallen between these numbers. Perhaps the best method for distinguishing the species is its overall coloration: darker and less brilliantly colored than the longear and having a dusky spot on each scale of the back and upper sides.

Not much is known of the habits of the dollar sunfish. It inhabits sluggish back waters and bayous to a greater extent than the longear sunfish. We have caught the dollar sunfish on hook-and-line in association with the warmouth, bluegill, spotted sunfish, largemouth bass, bantam sunfish, and longear. The dollar is strictly a southern species and occurs in bottomlands from South Carolina and Florida, to the eastern edge of Texas and the Red River floodplain of southeastern Oklahoma.

Bantam Sunfish

Lepomis symmetricus

Plate 141

Scientific name:
Lepomis, Greek for "scaled operculum"
symmetricus, Latin for "symmetrical," a reference to the lateral symmetry of the body

Distribution: Restricted to the south-central United States; mostly southeast Missouri, Arkansas, Louisiana, and east Texas.

Size: Adults average about 2 inches when fully grown; rarely growing as large as 3 or 4 inches.

Status: Of special concern or protected in Missouri, Kentucky, and Illinois.

The bantam sunfish is the smallest member of its genus and can be distinguished by its incomplete lateral line and the black spot in the base of the dorsal fin (present in young and most adults). This species inhabits heavily vegetated, stagnant waters, or slow-moving bayous and streams, where its principal associates include the warmouth, spotted sunfish, redear sunfish, pirate perch, flier, and largemouth bass. The entire distribution of the bantam sunfish stretches from southern Illinois and extreme southeastern Missouri south to western Mississippi and west to the eastern edge of Texas and southeastern Oklahoma.

Not much is known of the habits of this obscure little fish. They subsist on small crustaceans and insect larvae and probably help to control midge and mosquito populations to a minor extent. The bantam sunfish is a hardy species and is tolerant of low concentrations of oxygen. We have captured them in nets by the dozens in weedy swamps and bayous, which suggests that the species is loosely gregarious. Immature bantam sunfish typically sport bright orange pigment in their soft dorsal and anal fins. The bantam might be confused with the young of the spotted sunfish, although the latter species never has a dark spot in the base of its soft dorsal fin.

Hybrid Sunfishes

Plates 142–144

The similar behavior and ecological requirements of the sunfishes occasionally result in hybridization or "cross breeding." We have found in our collections in streams about 2 percent of the sunfishes to be hybrids. In nature, sunfishes tend to hybridize where one species is abundant and another is rare. Hybrids are typically intermediate in color, proportions, and whatever ways the parent species differ. The parent species of a hybrid can sometimes be ascertained by intermediate mouth size (particularly in the common cross between the bluegill and green sunfish), by color pattern, or by counting the lateral line scales of the hybrid. For instance, an orangespotted sunfish × green sunfish cross might be expected to have about 40 lateral line scales, a number that falls between the normal 41–52 range of the green sunfish and the 32–39 range of the orangespot. Hybrids can also be easily identified if one knows which sunfishes occur in a specific drainage. Hybrids are often sterile or have a reduced fecundity and greatly unbalanced sex ratios, so most hybrids will have had purebred progenitors. Fertile hybrids will sometimes "cross back" and breed with a pure species of sunfish, masking the identity of their offspring. Some hybrids are propagated for stocking because of their rapid growth, general good vigor, low fertility, and catchability. Stocked hybrids are of greatest utility in small ponds that are too small to support a balance of predators and prey. The hybrid's low reproductive capacity keeps populations low, and individual fish are usually larger as a result. Some of the popular hatchery hybrids include the green sunfish × redear (known as "hybrid bream" in Texas) and the bluegill × green sunfish (sometimes called "black perch").

Black Crappie

Pomoxis nigromaculatus

Plates 145–146

Colloquial names: calico bass, speckled perch, specks, slab, strawberry bass, grass bass, silver perch, white perch, tinmouth, bachelor, Mason perch, sac-a-lait, straw bass, bitterhead, bank-lick bass, lamplighter

Scientific name:
Pomoxis, Greek for "opercle sharp," the opercle ending in two sharp points, instead of an "earflap"
nigromaculatus, Latin for "black spotted"

Distribution: Throughout the eastern half of the United States except for the northeastern seaboard. Ranges farther north into Canada and deeper into the southeastern United States than does the white crappie. Widely stocked outside its native range.

Size: Reaching 12 inches and 1 pound, to a maximum of about 3 pounds. The world record is 6 lbs., from Westwego Canal in Louisiana, caught in 1969.

Status: Not threatened in any state.

The black crappie is a handsome fish with profusely speckled sides and is, on the average, slightly darker than its congeneric counterpart. Its random markings, deeper body, and seven or eight dorsal spines all help to distinguish it from the white crappie. The black crappie's striking contour of boldly patterned fins gave rise to its older common names of razorback and highfinned bass.

Like the white crappie, the male black crappie undergoes a change in color during the breeding season. In both species, the males become darker, developing blackened cheeks and belly and a brassy cast to the upper sides. When the water temperature reaches 56°F, male crappies begin building nests in shallow coves, during which time they are particularly accessible and vulnerable to anglers. The breeding and behavioral habits of the two crappies are similar, and the two species occasionally hybridize, producing the intermediate form "gray crappie."

At other times of the year, black crappie occur in loosely aggregated schools, whereby anglers catch them by the score with small, lead-headed crappie jigs or minnows. The crappie is not a vigorous fighter but is prized as food. Anglers generally "boat" crappies with the aid of a net or helping hand because the species' tender "papermouth" is susceptible to tearing. Both species cohabit streams and reservoirs, but the white crappie is usually the more abundant species in our region. The black crappie fares best over a firm bottom in cooler and clearer water and as a result is not very common in our larger and more turbid rivers.

Black crappies occasionally reach a weight of 2 pounds, and a few lakes consistently produce bigger fish. Growth of the black crappie is generally slower than that of the white, but because of its stockier body, a 10-inch black crappie weighs more than a white crappie of similar length. The black crappie is often better tasting than the white crappie, perhaps because of the black's preference for cleaner water.

White Crappie

Pomoxis annularis

Plate 147

Colloquial names: crappie, slab, silver perch, papermouth, sac-a-lait, tinmouth, barfish, bachelor, newlight, campbellite, speckled perch, bridge perch, white perch, John Demon, gold ring, timber crappie, shad

Scientific name:
Pomoxis, Greek for "opercle sharp," referring to the spiny, pointed gill cover
annularis, Latin for "having rings"

Distribution: Native to the Midwest and mid-south, now stocked throughout the continental United States.

Size: Commonly reaching 12 inches and 1 pound, to a maximum of about 3 pounds. The world record weighed 5 lbs. 3 oz. and was caught at Enid Dam, Mississippi, in July 1957.

Status: Not threatened in any state.

The hallmark of the white crappie is its sleek, graceful build and the beautiful subtle iridescence of its back and upper sides. As its name *annularis* implies, the white crappie is ringed with a series of regular vertical bands, although Rafinesque's original description of the species in 1818 referred to the golden ring that is sometimes present at the base of the tail. The crappie is also called gold ring for the ring around the pupil of its eye. The name *crappie* is derived from the Canadian-French word of *crapet* for the same species. Accordingly, the *a* in *crappie* is pronounced like the *a* in *walk*, thus averting an indelicate pronunciation! *Crapet* may have originated from the French *crêpe* for "pancake," which the general outline of the crappie does resemble, especially in the frying pan!

The white crappie is still known as campbellite in portions of Kentucky and Indiana, a title borrowed from the religious sect established by Alexander Campbell in the late 1820s. Members of the Campbellite sect were also known as the New Lights, as is the white crappie because of its brilliant sheen. The terms *campbellite* and *newlight* might have become interchangeable with the crappie as a result.

The white crappie is more tolerant of warm, turbid waters than the black crappie and is abundant in rivers, bayous, oxbows, and reservoirs. The white crappie has a predilection for flooded woodlands and waterlogged brush, particularly during the breeding season, hence the common appellation of timber crappie. Fisheries biologists enhance crappie fishing by sinking Christmas trees into reservoirs, thereby bringing the fish to the angler.

Flier

Centrarchus macropterus

Plate 148

Colloquial names: round flier, round sunfish, flying perch, perch, long-finned sunfish, shining bass, large-finned bass, many-spined sunfish, sac-a-lait

Scientific name:
Centrarchus, from the Greek *kentron* meaning "spine," and *archos* meaning "anus," a reference to the many anal fin spines
macropterus, Greek for "large fin"

Distribution: From Virginia and Florida to east Texas, northward in the Mississippi Valley lowland to southeast Missouri and southern Illinois.

Size: Up to 6 or 7 inches. Rarely growing to 1 pound or more. No official world record; the South Carolina record is 1 lb. 4 oz.

Status: Not threatened in any state.

The flier is a handsome, streamlined relative of the crappies, with all the subtle beauty of a shiny silver dollar. Its fins are garishly oversized, but their artful contours are a masterpiece of design. In its enthusiasm for floating insects, this sunfish sometimes bursts acrobatically through the surface of the water, a habit having earned it and its winglike fins the title of flier or flying perch.

The flier is strictly a lowland fish, occurring in swamps, bayous, and other weedy waters. It is most common in clean water with no noticeable current and is more tolerant of acidity than most other sunfishes. Although the flier is widespread throughout the south, it is not particularly abundant, and four or five adults might be considered a good day's catch. Because of the flier's tendency to rise to the surface, large adults are sporting when taken on a fly rod.

A young flier has a distinctive black spot (ocellus) ringed with orange in its soft dorsal fin. The "eye spot" is thought to focus a predator's attention, causing the pursuer to strike and give chase toward the fin and rear end of the fish, thus giving the flier a "head start" for escape. The flier is a slow-growing fish, and by its second summer of life is typically sexually mature, but only 3 inches long. Six- to 7-inch fish are usually four or five years old.

Perches and Darters

Family PERCIDAE

Well, sir, I had heard there is no better bait for a perch than a perch's eye. I adjusted that eye on the hook, and dropped in the line gently . . . in two minutes I saw that perch return. He approached the hook; he recognized his eye—frisked his tail—made a plunge—and, as I live, carried off the eye, safe and sound; and I saw him digesting it by the side of that water lily. The mocking fiend!
—*George Bulwer Lytton*
   My Novel

The perch family is a large and varied group that is distributed throughout much of Asia, Europe, and North America. Over 100 species are native to North America, including the yellow perch, the walleye and sauger, and the tiny darters. The darters are endemic to North America, but a close relative to the yellow perch is found in Europe, as are the zander (or pike-perch) and the berschick, the European equivalents of the sauger and walleye.

The perches are allied to the temperate basses, the sunfishes, and the drums but are not likely to be confused with them by anyone with even a passing interest in ichthyology. The long, streamlined body, one or two spines in the anal fin, and the separate dorsal fins all help to differentiate the perches from their relatives.

The perch family encompasses an array of habitats and a wide range of sizes. The walleye, being mostly a fish of lakes, is the largest of our percids, growing on occasion to 20 pounds. The sauger, which is mostly a denizen of rivers, is a little less pretentious than its lentic cousin and rarely exceeds a weight of 3 pounds. The darters, which comprise over 100 species, are most unusual of all. Bearing a resemblance to miniature sauger and walleye, most darters have a maximum length of 3 inches. During the breeding season, male darters are brightly cloaked in hues of blue, scarlet, orange, and green; they are among the most brilliantly colored of all North American fishes.

The sauger, walleye, and yellow perch are preeminent food fishes that are much sought after by anglers. Both walleye and yellow perch have supported commercial fisheries in the past, with much of the take coming from the Great Lakes.

Walleye

Stizostedion vitreum

Plate 149

Colloquial names: walleyed pike, pike-perch, yellow pike-perch, dory, glass eye, blue pike, gray pike, green pike, jack salmon, marble eye, yellow pickerel

Scientific name:
Stizostedion, Greek for "pungent throat," according to Rafinesque, who authored the genus, but the literal translation is "to prick a little breast"
vitreum, Latin for "glassy"

Distribution: Stocked into lakes throughout much of North America. Also common in the Missouri and upper Mississippi rivers and their larger tributaries.

Size: Commonly growing to 5 pounds and occasionally reaching 10–15 pounds. The world record walleye weighed 25 lbs. and was caught in August of 1960 from Old Hickory Lake in Tennessee.

Status: Of special concern in Mississippi.

The peculiar common name of walleye is an allusion to the large, glassy, "walleyed" pupils of this species. The ghostly stare of the walleye (and sauger) is a result of light reflected back through the pupil by crystalline matter in the retina, an anomaly that permits the walleye to see well in dark waters. Though often called pike-perch, yellow pike, or green pike, the walleye has no affinities with the true pikes, being in itself no more than an "overgrown perch." The nickname of "pike" is rooted in the outdated European name for the genus, *Lucioperca*, which when anglicized becomes *pike-perch*: the term *pike* for the walleye's long and slender form and *perch* in reference to its spiny perchlike dorsal fin. The extinct blue pike, a subspecies of the walleye (*Stizostedion vitreum glaucum*, not to be confused with the blue northern pike), was an important commercial species in Lake Erie prior to its elimination by severe pollution in the 1960s.

The walleye is a wanderer and during spring is known to migrate as far as 100 miles into tributary streams in search of suitable spawning sites. Walleyes will also spawn along rocky shores of lakes and the riprap of dams, where the cracks and crevices of the substrate serve to protect their adhesive eggs from predators. The walleye is exceptionally prolific, and females carry from 20,000 to 50,000 eggs per pound of body weight.

Walleyes prefer the deeper waters of lakes and large rivers but move into shallow flats to feed during early evening and night when their light-sensitive eyes afford them an advantage over their prey. The walleye is a good fighter on hook-and-line, though some of its accolades are probably contrived more from its sharp canine teeth and ferocious appearance than from its sportiness. Its gustatory virtues are considered to be first rate. The adult walleye is strictly carnivorous and eats mostly fishes. Forbes and Richardson in *The Fishes of Illinois* made the following extrapolations based on one specimen:

From a single wall-eyed pike caught in Peoria Lake, ten specimens of gizzard shad were taken, each from three to four inches long. . . . Reckoning the average life span of a pike at three years, the smallest reasonable estimate of food for each pike-perch would fall somewhere between eighteen hundred and three thousand fishes, and a hundred pike-perch such as should each year be taken along a few miles of a river like the Illinois would require 180,000 to 300,000 fishes for their food.

Sauger

Stizostedion canadense

Plate 150

Colloquial names: sand pike, gray pike, jack, jack salmon, river pike, spotfin pike, pickering, horsefish, spotted trout, rattlesnake pike

Scientific name:
Stizostedion, Greek for "pungent throat"
canadense, "from Canada"

Distribution: Throughout the larger rivers of the Mississippi River drainage, from Montana and Pennsylvania to northern Louisiana. Also common in the Great Lakes region, much of Canada, and the northeastern United States.

Size: Growing to 18 inches and 3 or 4 pounds. The world record sauger of 8 lbs. 12 oz. was caught from Lake Sakakawea, North Dakota, in October 1971.

Status: Sport fish; of special concern in Mississippi.

The sauger sports the same "glassy stare" as and is the lotic congener of the walleye. The sauger, typically shorter and more slender than the walleye, is most abundant in our larger rivers and in a few northern lakes where it has been stocked. The sauger can be identified by its dark brown saddle blotches and by the distinct rows of spots in its dorsal fin, whereas the walleye is trademarked by the white tip on its tail and the dark membranes in the posterior end of the spiny dorsal fin. Identification of the sauger and walleye is confounded by an artificial hybrid called a *saugeye*. Faded, or even fresh, saugeye can sometimes appear as wholly indistinct from the walleye. Constantine Rafinesque, who described the genus *Stizostedion* in 1820, apparently did not distinguish between the sauger and walleye, and his account of the Salmon Perch from the Ohio River includes diagnostic characteristics of both species.

The sauger is known colloquially as rattlesnake pike, probably in allusion to the flat, snakelike head of the sand pike—a subspecies of sauger native to the Upper Missouri River. Like the walleye and yellow perch, the sauger has a voracious appetite and feeds primarily on fishes and crayfish. Anglers go "saugering" during the upstream spawning runs in spring when sauger migrate into smaller tributaries or become trapped below navigation dams. Sauger are tolerant of turbid waters and provide an excellent fishery in the Missouri and Mississippi rivers, where they usually occur with the less abundant walleye.

Yellow Perch

Perca flavescens
Plate 151

Colloquial names: ring perch, perch, lake perch, redfin perch, convict, raccoon perch, coontail, yellow ned, striped perch

Scientific name:
Perca, Greek for "perch"
flavescens, Latin for "yellowish"

Distribution: Primarily in the northeastern United States; also common in southern Canada. Most abundant in our region in northern Iowa, Minnesota, and the Dakotas.

Size: Adults range from 6 to 12 inches, up to 1 or 2 pounds. The world record yellow perch of 4 lbs. 3 oz. was caught by the famous naturalist Charles C. Abbott, M.D., from Crosswicks Creek, New Jersey, in May 1865—the longest standing angling record in North America!

Status: Sport fish; of special concern in Kentucky.

The yellow perch is probably the most abundant and well-known species of panfish in the northeastern United States. Although it is occasionally found in the sluggish pools of rivers, the yellow perch abounds in cold, clear ponds or lakes as the vernacular lake perch implies.

Young yellow perch live near shore, where they are often seen schooling among the weeds, dock pilings, or rocky reefs. The adults will usually retreat to deeper, cooler water during the summer, returning to the shallows during evening to feed. In ponds and smaller lakes with few large predators, yellow perch are often stunted, earning for their waters the derogatory designation of "perch lake."

"It is a true fish," wrote Henry David Thoreau of the perch, "such as the angler loves to put into his basket or hang on top of his willow twig on shady afternoons, along the banks of the streams." Yellow perch are carnivorous and simple to catch. Worms or small minnows make ideal baits, but perch will nibble at anything that feigns edibility.

The perch is generally touted to be an excellent food, but its taste is contingent on the quality of its water and the season of the year. Even the gourmand ichthyologist David Starr Jordan had disparate opinions. "The flesh of the yellow perch is much inferior to that of the bass or pike-perches, being rather soft, coarse and insipid," wrote Jordan in 1882; only to overturn his verdict by the turn of the century, saying "As a panfish we do not know of any better among American freshwater fishes."

The yellow perch has an apocryphal cousin, the "black-dotted perch," with a genealogy traceable to one John James Audubon. Audubon presented a drawing of the mythical fish to C. S. Rafinesque as part of an elaborate practical joke, and Rafinesque described the fish in 1820 as a new species, *Perca nigropunctata*!

Darters

Percina spp.

Plates 152–153

Scientific name:

Percina, Greek for "a small perch"

Distribution: Eastern United States and Canada, with most species occurring east of the Great Plains.

Size: Usually 2–4 inches, except the logperch, which grows to 7–8 inches. According to David Starr Jordan " . . . the most of a fish, and therefore the least of a darter."

Status: Several species are threatened or of special concern in the central United States.

There are about 30 species of darters in the genus *Percina*, and 13 of these occur in the central United States. Among our more widely distributed species are the blackside darter, dusky darter, the logperch, and the slenderhead darter. The percinid darters are typically larger fish than darters in the genera *Etheostoma* and *Ammocrypta* and also have better developed gas bladders. This improved buoyancy permits them to spend more time in mid-water off the stream bottom. Several of the percinid darters prefer sluggish pools and runs in lieu of the more typical riffle-bottom habitat, but all feed primarily on invertebrates that they root from the streambed. The large snouts of several species of *Percina*, including the conical "pig-nose" of the logperch (or hogfish), are used to turn over small stones, which the darters then thoroughly search for invertebrates.

Spawning behavior of many darters in this genus is poorly known. In some species, the eggs are apparently scattered over gravel riffles, but the female logperch will deposit and fertilize her eggs while vibrating her body and burying herself into sand or gravel riffles.

The logperch is large enough to be caught on hook-and-line, a practice that Jordan and Evermann ascribed as being of principal utility to "urchins." Logperch so caught are sometimes gutted and fried whole and are said to be very tasty. Several species of *Percina* are threatened or of special concern in the United States, including the bigscale logperch, blackside darter, and the endangered leopard darter.

Darters

Etheostoma spp.

Plates 154–160

Scientific name:
Etheostoma, from the Greek *etheo*, "to strain" and *stoma*, "mouth." Said by Rafin-esque to mean "various mouths." Jordan and Evermann suggest the name might have been intended as *Heterostoma*," for "different mouths."

Distribution: Eastern United States and adjacent areas of Canada; most species within forested regions east of the Great Plains.

Size: Most species 1.5–3 inches, but a few reach 5–6 inches maximum length.

Status: Many species are federally threat-ened or endangered, and several species are protected in states within the central United States.

The genus *Etheostoma* is composed of about 90 species of darters, all of which are native to North America, and about 30 of which occur in the central United States. Many of these species have limited distributions and are protected by law (e.g., Arkansas darter and greenthroat darter), but three species are relatively widespread, especially to the north and onto the Great Plains: the Iowa darter, johnny darter, and orangethroat darter. Each species of darter has its own habitat preference and most live in streams, but as a group darters occupy a wide range of habitats from clear headwater springs to swampy bayous and lowland lakes.

The *Etheostoma* darters have poorly de-veloped gas bladders and are consequently nonbuoyant, spending most of their time on gravelly bottoms where they live up to the names *darter* and *perch* by darting about from one perching site to another. Although most darters spend the majority of their time on the bottom, species such as the Ar-kansas darter and least darter prefer to rest among the underwater "forests" of fila-mentous algae and submerged vascular plants. All darters are thought to feed on aquatic insects and other small inverte-brates.

Reproductive behavior among the darters varies with the species. Male johnny darters and fantail darters claim cavities beneath rocks as their hatcheries. A female will swim from stone to stone until she finds a male at home, whereupon she enters and deposits a layer of eggs on the ceiling of the den. The male remains in the den to clean and aerate the eggs. The fleshy, knob-tipped spines on the dorsal fin of the fantail darter seem to be specially adapted for this purpose. Orangethroat darters and rainbow darters bury their eggs in the gravel, with the female "bulldozing" head first into the substrate until her upper body is reexposed above the bottom. The territorial male then moves above her, and both vibrate rapidly to help fertilize and bury the eggs. Other darters, including the greenside and least darters, attach their eggs to submerged veg-etation.

During their breeding season, male dart-ers are among the most beautifully colored of all freshwater fishes. Although their pig-mentation is not quite as intense or as long lasting as that of some tropical fishes, the docile, inquisitive personality of darters and the ease with which they are cared for make them an enjoyable addition to any aquar-ium with native fishes.

The darters are also supposedly good for food, according to nineteenth-century naturalist Constantine Rafinesque, who wrote of the johnny darters, "they are good to eat, fried." To which David Starr Jordan later added: "This is doubtless true, but I should as soon think of filling my pan with wood warblers. The good man goes a-fishing not for 'pot-luck' but to let escape the Indian within him."

Drums

Family SCIAENIDAE

*Another still larger, noticed as a great haul of
Drum-fish: "On Wednesday, June 5, 1804,"
says the postmaster of Oyster Ponds, Long
Island, "one seine drew on shore at this place at
a single haul 12,250 fish, the average weight of
which was found to be thirty-three pounds,
making in the aggregate 202 tons 250 pounds.
This undoubtedly is the greatest haul of this
kind ever known in this country. A hundred
witnesses are ready to attest the truth of the
above statement. They are used for manure."
(The fish, I suppose, and not the witnesses,
remarked Ingersoll.)*
—George Brown Goode
    American Fishes

Freshwater Drum

Aplodinotus grunniens

Plate 161

Colloquial names: white perch, sheeps-head, gaspergou (in Louisiana), goo, croaker, thunderpumper, crocus, silver bass, gray perch, lake drum, jewel-head, grunt, bubbler, grinder, river drum

Scientific name:
Aplodinotus, Greek for "single back," reference to the slightly joined dorsal fins
grunniens, Latin for "grunting"

Distribution: Occurring from south-central Canada and the Great Lakes to Mexico. Absent from the East Coast.

Size: Commonly reaching 5 pounds and occasionally as large as 15 pounds. In the 1800s, 40–60 pound fish were common-place. The world record, caught in Nicka-jack Lake, Tennessee, in 1972, weighed 54 lbs. 8 oz.

Status: Not threatened in any state.

The sciaenids are a large, cosmopolitan family of coastal marine fishes with great commercial importance, including such typified seagoers as the red drum, the weakfishes, and croakers. The freshwater drum is the only widespread species of this family in the fresh waters of the United States, although the red drum has been introduced as a sport fish into several Texas reservoirs, including the warm-water Lake Braunig near San Antonio. The freshwater drum has the distinction of having the greatest latitudinal distribution (native range) of any freshwater sport fish in our region; it occurs from central Manitoba to the Yucatan Peninsula in Mexico.

The freshwater drum is a denizen of rivers, natural lakes, and reservoirs, where it feeds along the bottoms upon immature insects, crayfish, and minnows. The throat teeth of the drum are broad and heavy and especially well adapted to crushing mollusks, on which it sometimes feeds. The odd colloquial name of gaspergou is derived from the Louisiana-French *casburgot* and is equivalent to the French *casser*, "to break," and *burgeau*, a kind of shellfish.

The drum earned the specific epithet *grunniens* for its peculiar drumming or "grunting" noises, produced by a special set of muscles that are vibrated against the swim bladder. Spawning of the freshwater drum has not been observed by scientists, but the "grunting" sounds are associated with spring and early summer migrations and might be a ritual of breeding.

The otoliths or "ear bones" of the freshwater drum are unusually large and have a texture like ivory. In the center of each otolith is an indentation that looks not unlike the letter *L*; this has probably given rise to their being called lucky stones. The otoliths are sometimes carried as amulets and were formerly prized by young boys who collected them from fish scraps heaped by commercial fishermen.

Cichlids

Family CICHLIDAE

*It is of interest to note that the habit of these
Cichlids of congregating in shoals at the surface
leaves them open to the attacks of the myriads of
Crested Grebes that abound in this region. . . .
The birds are in the habit of snatching at the
most tasty morsel, the eyes, lifting out the
eyeballs and the infra-orbital partition with a
single stroke of their long, sharp beaks. This
does not always cause the death of the victim,
and many members of the shoals may be
observed to be flourishing in a condition of
absolute blindness.*
—J. R. Norman
    A History of Fishes

Rio Grande Perch

Cichlasoma cyanoguttatum

Plate 162

Colloquial names: Texas cichlid, blue-spotted perch, guinea perch

Scientific name:
Cichlasoma, Greek for "body of a wrasse," a similar type of fish
cyanoguttatum, Greek for "blue spotted"

Distribution: Northeastern Mexico and sporadically in the southern third of Texas, principally in the Rio Grande system and where introduced in the Edwards Plateau.

Size: Generally 5–6 inches in length, to a maximum of 10 inches.

Status: Sport fish; not threatened.

The cichlids comprise a large and varied family of fishes that consists mostly of tropical freshwater fishes. Cichlids abound in Central and South America and in Africa, and a few species are native to Asia. The cichlid family includes a number of popular warm-water aquarium fishes such as the angelfish, oscar, and Jack Dempsey. The Rio Grande perch is the only cichlid native to the United States, where it occurs in the warm, subtropical waters of southern Texas.

The Rio Grande perch superficially resembles the sunfishes but differs in several obvious respects as well as in skeletal structure. The cichlids have only one nostril on each side of the head, instead of two, and the Rio Grande perch has an interrupted lateral line that is doubled for a short distance on the caudal peduncle.

The strong, cutting teeth of the Rio Grande perch make it chiefly carnivorous, and it feeds mostly on fish eggs, insects, and small fishes. Because of a high rate of reproduction, this species often overpopulates impoundments and competes with more desirable panfishes for food and space. The species is a popular panfish in Mexico, where it is an important source of protein.

Seasonally cool water restricts the spread of the Rio Grande perch to the north. Along the outskirts of its northern limits in the Edwards Plateau, the Rio Grande perch can survive the cool winters only in the "cooling lakes" of power plants or in rivers near the outlets of warm springs.

Sculpins

Family COTTIDAE

*Now the Sculpin is a little water beast which
pretends to consider itself a fish, and, under that
pretext, hangs about the piles on which West
Boston Bridge is built, swallowing the bait and
hook intended for flounders. On being drawn
from the water, it exposes an immense head, a
diminutive bony carcass, and a surface so full of
spines, ridges, ruffles and frills that the
naturalists have not been able to count them
without quarreling about their number.*
—Oliver Wendell Holmes
     The Professor at the Breakfast Table

Sculpins

Cottus

Plate 163

Colloquial names: muddler, miller's thumb, spoonhead, blob, cockatouch

Scientific name:
Cottus, old Greek name for European miller's thumb

Distribution: In our region primarily in the Ozarks of southern Missouri, Arkansas, and northeast Oklahoma. The mottled sculpin is also found in extreme southeast Minnesota, northeast Iowa, and the central Rocky Mountains.

Size: Usually 2.5–4.5 inches. Banded sculpin up to 7 inches.

Status: The banded sculpin is of special concern in Kansas and Mississippi.

The sculpins are principally marine fishes and include some 300 species worldwide, but the genus *Cottus* includes many freshwater species in North America, Europe, and Asia. Sculpins are slick, smooth-bodied fishes that lack scales and are indicative of clean, unpolluted waters. The broad, flat head and oversized pectoral fins of the sculpin give it a distinctive, somewhat grotesque profile. The sculpin's generic nickname of miller's thumb supposedly refers to the similarity between the sculpin and the thumb of a miller who had his digit smashed between millstones.

Four species occur within the central United States: the mottled sculpin, Ozark sculpin, banded sculpin, and slimy sculpin. These species typically inhabit clean, cool headwater streams in our region. They feed primarily on invertebrates and are also predaceous on trout eggs; however, sculpins probably eat only those eggs that are not properly covered by gravel and are loose on the surface. Sculpins are seldom harmful to trout populations and can be an important forage species for trouts. The banded sculpin and other freshwater sculpins are camouflaged by a protective pigmentation system that allows them to blend in with their surroundings. Their quick, darting movements and motionless postures make the sculpins inconspicuous to any but the keenest of observers.

Male sculpins shape their nests under flat rocks or in cavities along stream banks. Some of our freshwater sculpins spawn in a topsy-turvy fashion, turning themselves upside-down, whereby the female deposits her eggs on the ceiling of the nest. Sculpins are cannibalistic, but males defend their eggs and fry, sometimes employing a silent warning behavior that ichthyologist William J. Koster once likened to the "barking" motions of a dog.

Selected Bibliography

Bailey, Reeve M., and Marvin O. Allum. 1962. Fishes of South Dakota. Misc. Pub. Mus. Zool., Univ. Mich. No. 119. 131 pp.

Baxter, George T., and James R. Simon. 1970. Wyoming Fishes. Wyoming Game and Fish Dept. Bull. 4. 168 pp.

Becker, George C. 1983. Fishes of Wisconsin. University of Wisconsin Press: Madison. 1052 pp.

Berg, L. S. 1949. Freshwater Fishes of the U.S.S.R. and Adjacent Countries, Vols. 1–3, 4th ed. Izdatel'stvo Akademii Nauk SSR: Moskva-Leningrad. Translated from Russian by Israel Program for Scientific Translations: Jerusalem, 1964.

Blatchley, William S. 1938. The Fishes of Indiana. The Nature Publishing Company: Indianapolis. 121 pp.

Brown, C. J. D. 1971. Fishes of Montana. Big Sky Books, Montana State University: Bozeman. 207 pp.

Brown's Angler's Almanac. 1848, 1849, 1851. John J. Brown & Co.: New York.

Buchanan, Thomas M. 1973. Key to the Fishes of Arkansas. Arkansas Game and Fish Commission: Little Rock. 68 pp. + 198 maps.

Caine, Lou S. 1949. North American Fresh Water Sport Fish. A. S. Barnes & Co.: New York. 212 pp.

Carson, Rachel L. 1944. Food from Home Waters: Fishes of the Middle West. U.S. Dept. Interior, Fish and Wildlife Service, Conservation Bull. 34. 44 pp.

Cashner, Robert C., and Royal D. Suttkus. 1977. *Ambloplites constellatus*, a new species of rock bass from the Ozark Upland of Arkansas and Missouri with a review of western rock bass populations. Amer. Midl. Nat. 98:147–161.

Clay, William M. 1975. The Fishes of Kentucky. Kentucky Department of Fish and Wildlife Resources: Frankfort. 416 pp.

Cross, Frank B. 1967. Handbook of Fishes of Kansas. Univ. Kansas Mus. Nat. Hist., Misc. Publ. 45:1–357.

Cross, Frank B., and Joseph T. Collins. 1975. Fishes in Kansas. Univ. Kansas Mus. Nat. Hist., Publ. Educ. Ser. No. 3. 189 pp.

Douglas, Neil H. 1974. Freshwater Fishes of Louisiana. Claitor's Publishing Division: Baton Rouge. 443 pp.

Eddy, Samuel, and James C. Underhill. 1974. Northern Fishes, 3d ed. University of Minnesota Press: Minneapolis. 414 pp.

———. 1978. How to Know the Freshwater Fishes, 3d ed. William C. Brown Co. Publishers: Dubuque, IA. 215 pp.

Forbes, Stephen A., and R. E. Richardson. 1920. The Fishes of Illinois, 2d ed. St. Illinois Nat. Hist. Surv. Div. 357 pp.

Goode, George B. 1888. American Fishes. Standard Book Co.: New York.

Gowanloch, James Nelson. 1933. Fishes and Fishing in Louisiana. Department of Conservation: State of Louisiana. 638 pp.

Harlan, James R., E. B. Speaker, and James Mayhew. 1987. Iowa Fish and Fishing. Iowa Department of Natural Resources: Des Moines. 323 pp.

Heckman, William L. 1950. Steamboating; Sixty-five Years on Missouri's Rivers. Burton Publishing Co.: Kansas City, MO. 284 pp.

Henshall, James A. 1881. Book of the Black Bass. R. Clarke & Co.: Cincinnati. 463 pp.

Hubbs, Carl L., and Reeve M. Bailey. 1940. A revision of the black basses, (*Micropterus* and *Huro*) with descriptions of four new forms. Misc. Publ. Mus. Zool., Univ. Michigan, No. 48:1–51.

———. 1942. Subspecies of spotted bass (*Micropterus punctulatus*) in Texas. Occ. Papers Mus. Zool., Univ. Michigan, No. 457:1–11.

Hubbs, Carl L., and K. F. Lagler. 1964. Fishes of the Great Lakes Region. University of Michigan Press: Ann Arbor. 213 pp.

Hunter, J. R., and A. D. Hasler. 1965. Spawning association of the redfin shiner, *Notropis umbratilis*, and the green sunfish, *Lepomis cyanellus*. Copeia 1965:265–281.

Johnson, James E. 1987. Protected Fishes of the United States and Canada. American Fisheries Society: Bethesda, MD. 42 pp.

Jordan, David Starr, and Barton W. Evermann. 1902. American Food and Game Fishes. Doubleday, Page & Co.: New York. 573 pp.

———. 1896–1900. Fishes of North and Middle America. Bull. U.S. Nat. Mus. 47(1–4): 3313 pp. + 392 pls.

Jordan, D. S., B. W. Evermann, and H. Walton Clark. 1930. Check List of the Fishes and Fishlike Vertebrates of North and Middle America. Report of the U.S. Fish Commission for the Fiscal Year 1928. 670 pp.

Kemp, Robert J., Jr., 1971. Freshwater Fishes of Texas. Texas Parks and Wildlife Department: Austin. 40 pp.

Koster, William J. 1957. Guide to the Fishes of New Mexico. University of New Mexico Press: Albuquerque. 116 pp.

Lee, David S., Carter R. Gilbert, Charles H. Hocutt, Robert E. Jenkins, Don E. McAllister, and Jay R. Stauffer, Jr. 1980 et seq. Atlas of North American Freshwater Fishes. North Carolina State Museum of Natural History: Raleigh. 867 pp.

Miller, Rudolph J., and Henry W. Robison. 1973. The Fishes of Oklahoma. Oklahoma State University Press: Stillwater. 246 pp.

Minckley, W. L. 1973. Fishes of Arizona. Arizona Game and Fish Department: Phoenix. 293 pp.

Morris, Jerry, Larry Morris, and Larry Witt. 1972. The Fishes of Nebraska. Nebraska Game and Parks Commission: Lincoln. 98 pp.

Moyle, Peter B. 1976. Inland Fishes of California. University of California Press: Berkeley. 405 pp.

Norman, J. R. 1931. A History of Fishes. Frederick A. Stokes Co.: New York. 463 pp.

Norman, J. R., and P. H. Greenwood. 1963. A History of Fishes, 2d ed. Ernest Benn Ltd.: London. 398 pp.

Paetz, Martin J., and Joseph S. Nelson. 1970. The Fishes of Alberta. The Queen's Printer: Edmonton. 281 pp.

Pflieger, William L. 1975. The Fishes of Missouri. Missouri Department of Conservation: Jefferson City. 343 pp.

Phillips, Gary L., William D. Schmid, and James C. Underhill. 1982. Fishes of the Minnesota Region. University of Minnesota Press: Minneapolis. 248 pp.

Rafinesque, Constantine Samuel. 1820. Ichthyologia Ohiensis, or Natural History of the Fishes Inhabiting the River Ohio and Its Tributary Streams. W. G. Hunt: Lexington, KY. 90 pp.

Robins, C. Richard, Reeve M. Bailey, Carl E. Bond, James R. Brooker, Ernest A. Lachner, Robert N. Lea, and W. B. Scott. 1980. A List of Common and Scientific Names of Fishes from the United States and Canada, 4th ed. American Fisheries Society: Bethesda, MD. Spec. Publ. No. 12:1–174.

Robison, Henry W., and Thomas M. Buchanan. 1988. Fishes of Arkansas. University of Arkansas Press: Fayetteville. 536 pp.

Roosevelt, Robert Barnwell. 1862. Game Fish of the Northern States of America and British Provinces. Carleton: New York. 324 pp.

Scott, W. B., and E. J. Crossman. 1973. Freshwater Fishes of Canada. Fisheries Research Board of Canada, Bull. No. 184. 966 pp.

Smith, Philip W. 1979. The Fishes of Illinois. University of Illinois Press: Urbana. 314 pp.

Sublette, James E., Michael D. Hatch, and Mary Sublette. In prep. Fishes of New Mexico. University of New Mexico Press: Albuquerque.

Thoreau, Henry David. 1963. The Portable Thoreau, rev. ed. Carl Bode, ed. Viking Press: New York. 698 pp.

Trautman, Milton B. 1981. The Fishes of Ohio,

rev. ed. Ohio State University Press: Columbus. 782 pp.

Walton, Izaak. 1906. The Compleat Angler. J. M. Dent and Co.: London. 215 pp.

Woodling, John. 1980. Game Fish of Colorado. Colorado Division of Wildlife: Denver. 40 pp.

———. 1985. Colorado's Little Fish. Colorado Division of Wildlife: Denver. 77 pp.

Index

Numbers in italics refer to the color plates.